A SAPPER OFFICER'S WAR 1915–1917

A SAPPER OFFICER'S WAR 1915–1917

THE MEMOIRS OF RALPH A. BAGNOLD, FOUNDER OF THE LONG RANGE DESERT GROUP IN WORLD WAR TWO

RALPH A. BAGNOLD

EDITED BY CHRISTOPHER RALPH BAGNOLD

FRONTLINE
BOOKS

A SAPPER OFFICER'S WAR 1915–1917
From WW2 into the Cold War

First published in Great Britain in 2026
by Frontline Books
An imprint of
Pen & Sword Books Ltd
Yorkshire - Philadelphia

ISBN 9781036181741

A CIP catalogue record for this book is available from the British Library

Typeset by Lapiz Digital
Printed and bound in the UK by CPI Group (UK) Ltd,
Croydon, CR0 4YY.

Printed on paper from a sustainable source by
CPI Group (UK) Ltd, Croydon, CR0 4YY

The Publisher's authorised representative in the EU for product safety is Authorised Rep Compliance Ltd., Ground Floor, 71 Lower Baggot Street, Dublin D02 P593, Ireland.
www.arccompliance.com

For a complete list of Pen & Sword titles please contact
PEN & SWORD BOOKS LTD
47 Church Street, Barnsley, South Yorkshire, S70 2AS, England
E-mail: enquiries@pen-and-sword.co.uk
Website: www.pen-and-sword.co.uk
or
PEN & SWORD BOOKS
1950 Lawrence Rd, Havertown, PA 19083, USA
E-mail: uspen-and-sword@casematepublishers.com

CONTENTS

FOREWORD
by Christopher Ralph Bagnold

My grandfather, Ralph Alger Bagnold – scientist, desert explorer and founder of the Long Range Desert Group in the Second World War – was born in 1896. In the summer of 1914 as he left school war broke out in Europe and, like many young men caught up in the groundswell of the times, he joined the army of his country. Having attended Malvern College and coming from a military family (his father was a British Army colonel) R.A.B.[1] became an officer cadet almost automatically, choosing as his regiment the Royal Engineers.[2] After training at the Royal Military Academy in Woolwich, he stepped ashore in France in July 1915 as a 19-year-old subaltern and was to serve on the Western Front until the Armistice in 1918.

Being an engineer, R.A.B. was typically billeted several miles behind the front line, moving up each night to work in the trenches and in no man's land. In 1915 and the first half of 1916, his unit (the 83rd Field Company[3] attached to the 20th Division[4]) was based at Laventie in France and then at Ypres in Belgium but in July 1916, carried by the momentum of the times, they marched southwards to the Somme. The four chapters detailing his experiences on the Somme are the lynchpin of the memoir. Initially struck by the vastness of the enterprise and hopeful of success, R.A.B.'s perspective begins to change and, as the enormous offensive drags on, he starts to comprehend the impossibility of a decisive victory in 1916. He also begins to think of his own prospects and wonders how long his good fortune will hold. Early in September 1916 near Guillemont he casually remarks, 'For the most part we were extraordinarily lucky.' Very much against the odds he was never physically wounded.

In 1919, R.A.B. gathered his memories and written notes into a single narrative. This was initially a handwritten account that was then typed up into two copies by a proficient corporal. These volumes, with stout covers, thick paper and accompanying maps and photographs (the latter, stock images sourced by R.A.B. from the Imperial War Museum) are treasured family possessions and until recently were the only complete written records of R.A.B.'s memoirs. I decided to put these pages into digital form and as I typed away, I began to ponder how widely R.A.B. wished them to be read. To my knowledge, he never sought their publication, although in his autobiography *Sand, Wind and War* (published 1990), R.A.B. did include a succinct chapter entitled 'France and Flanders 1915–1918.' The fact that he had given his 'First War' experiences autobiographical coverage (he always called it the 'First War') indicates a desire to connect with a broader audience, and the opening line of the preface to the memoirs that follow here also identifies a strong wish to share:

> All the time I've been in France, I've had one great longing, an impossible one. To take some friend or near relation who has lived at home, to transport him suddenly to the Front some dark, nasty night and show him the war as it really was.

Despite the literal impossibility of that wish, I feel this 1915-1917 memoir achieves something like it. He tells us of people and of comradeship – the cosy gatherings in tiny mess dugouts and the bonhomie among his working parties. There are horrible things too: he writes of the big fat rats and the flies that swarm over decaying bodies with their lingering stench like rotten cheese. He partially inhales poisonous gas and wonders how long the pain in his chest will last. He witnesses military innovation, seeing the first tanks arrive at the Front and noting the new practice of the 'creeping' artillery barrage. Sometimes the narrative resonates with more widely known texts. His description of being under attack from a heavy trench mortar anticipates Robert Graves' description of the same in *Goodbye to All That* and Erich Remarque's observation in *All Quiet on the Western Front* about soldiers regarding the earth as a familiar friend also resonates with R.A.B.'s sapper officer perspective: 'All our work was in the earth. It was the one great idea in our minds.'

During an interview for the Imperial War Museum recorded shortly before his death in 1990, R.A.B. was asked, 'What was the feeling of you and your brother officers towards the Germans? Did you hate them or respect them?' He replied, 'Oh they were just the Bosch. I suppose one didn't think about them, except as an enemy.' In spite of his use of the term 'Bosch' – which to the modern reader will probably sound pejorative – there was no animosity in his voice and there is no notable ill-feeling towards the Germans in these pages.

However, there *is* a growing undercurrent of odium in the memoir and the finger points squarely at the men directing the war from châteaux far behind the lines. Siegfried Sassoon famously 'cursed the staff as incompetent swine' in his poem 'The General', and while I never heard R.A.B. openly challenge a figure of authority, he does criticise the staff in these pages and identifies these feelings as widespread: 'There was bitter feeling against them. It was a feeling, I suppose, very much like that at home between the very poor and the very rich.' The German Commander Ludendorff's remark that the British troops were 'lions led by donkeys'[5] seems to ring true here and one is reminded of other notorious remarks, such as that attributed to Kiggel, Haig's Chief of Staff: 'Good God. Did we really send men to fight in that?'[6] But of course, fighting in '*that*' is what they did. Towards the end of his Somme chapter, R.A.B. recounts the time when he and his men, on night-time engineering work in open ground, find themselves under sustained and accurately ranged shellfire.

> It seemed impossible that anyone could live through this until morning. It was the only time I can remember when I really felt I shouldn't ever get back again. […] Suddenly there was a shriek, and a blazing yellow flame that seemed to fill the whole universe. Then everything began to spin round with a great singing noise, and I found myself lying on the ground with a rain of hot earth still falling on me. I picked myself up and went on. There was a great noise in my head and a curious indifference to what happened to me. The shells bursting all round seemed to mean nothing. But I was terrified that something should happen inside, that I should suddenly run away into the darkness.

Of all the lines in the memoir this last one perhaps comes closest to a feeling of abject terror and a sense that he would break. But he doesn't and the narrative immediately steadies and shows us how soldiers carry on and see each other through: 'A few minutes later I came across Ruddle again. He was just the same as ever, cheery and apparently quite unperturbed.'

It seems a little odd that the memoir ends so abruptly and arguably incompletely in August 1917 with the following phrase:

> Sometimes in the early morning as the lorry took us back along the St. Jean Road down the gentle hill past battery after battery of guns, one could see the gas in the dim dawn, hanging near the ground and slowly pouring like a grey oil down the hill from shell hole to shell hole, where the batteries had been shelled during the night.

I see this final picture of desolation as something like a Paul Nash's painting from the latter part of the war, and the described scene clearly marks the point at which R.A.B. the writer had had enough. I also see this ending as entirely fitting – like a life cut suddenly short – and feel that like so many wartime narratives this one was in some way written inadvertently on behalf of the countless number who did not come back. A memorial to shared experience and a gift to the receptive reader.

Christopher Ralph Bagnold,
April 2026

Preface

REMINISCENCES, 1919

All the time I've been in France, I've had one great longing, an impossible one. To take some friend or near relation who has lived at home, to transport him suddenly to the Front some dark, nasty night and show him the war as it really was. I think that more than half what we call romance is the anticipation, however unrealisable, of being able afterwards to talk about and make people picture what one has seen and done and been through. How often have we thought of someone in England and said to ourselves, 'If only he or she was here now watching this.'

Now it's all gone and can never be reproduced. There is no real record of it except a mental one which can't be duplicated or copied at all. All the places I have such vivid pictures of in my mind no longer exist as I saw them. The ground has become more or less natural again, grass has grown, the trenches have fallen in, and the people, the sounds and the smells have all gone. Directly the Armistice came, everything seemed to drop out of life. The whole spirit of the thing died: that wonderful unconscious spirit of being part of one gigantic machine that was working for one purpose. The purpose suddenly disappeared.

When one actually tries to describe some incident, one realises how impossible it is ever to make anyone see things as one saw them oneself.

I wish I'd kept the diary I started when I first went out. I did keep it up for the first five months [July–December 1915], but it gradually faded away, got more and more behind and finally dropped out altogether. It was very hard to keep a diary. There wasn't time for one thing. Besides, for long periods no one liked going over the events of the day before. It was only one step from that to thinking of having to do the same thing the next day, and that was fatal.

Introduction

FIRST EXPERIENCES (JULY–SEPTEMBER 1915)

20th July 1915

Well, we landed in France at about 9.30 am on the morning of 20th July 1915. There were seven of us from Chatham: Grindley and Perrott and five Canadians. Grindley always used to beat me for top place in the form at school. We were all very thrilled with getting to France, and full of ourselves as sapper officers. I had very vague notions about the war. I don't think I can have read papers at all while I was at the Shop[7] or at Chatham. I only knew vaguely where the Front[8] was. It was all France. As long as you were in France, you were in it all right. We had absolutely no picture in our minds of what it was like up there.

That night we left for Rouen. It was our first experience of a journey in a military train in France. Every quarter of an hour the train would stop for no apparent reason and then crawl on again. It didn't reach Rouen until eight or nine the next morning.

At Rouen we reported to the RTO[9] who inspired us with awe and were told to go on to No.[10] 4 General Base Depot. We could leave our kit at the station and a lorry would fetch it.

I think that depot was typical of them all except that it was only for Royal Engineers. It was all huts and tents. The only large permanent huts were the mess, the orderly room, and the QM[11] store. Just around the mess were about thirty 'Armstrong' huts of stretched canvas for the officers, and beyond these the main camp lay in line after line of tents. All the way up the hill out of the town to the camp there were other depots full of infantry, cavalry, and Indians.

There was nothing on Earth to do except censor the men's letters, write letters and wander about the town. We had had a course at

Chatham on hutting[12] and after a fortnight we were so bored we tried to get jobs with the RE Works' Company who were still putting up more and more huts. Anything was better than doing nothing in the depot.

We discovered that this wasn't France after all. The war was still as far away as ever, or very nearly. On a few nights we could just see the flashes of the guns very faintly and we longed to be up there, to be in it. The war might be over before we had seen it. There were several officers in the mess who had come down from the line, wounded or gassed or something else and who were waiting to go back again. We wanted to go too. How long would we stay here? Why didn't they send us to field companies straight away? Perhaps we had been forgotten about.

There were several most interesting officers in the mess. There was Captain Wellesley who had done the mining of Hill 60 just before the Second Battle of Ypres, and a man from one of the new mining companies who had been gassed and blown up somewhere 'up there'.

The depot was at that time full of miners and chemists. There was a boom in mining, just then, and new companies were being formed all along the Front. The mess was full of mining officers, mostly experts from abroad, who'd been at Chatham for a month or so and come straight out to France. The old hands like Macnamara used to spin yarns about 'up the line' and all the other new fellows would sit and listen rather in awe.

The chemists were something quite new and awfully hush-hush. They were the pioneers in frightfulness [*sic*] reprisals. It was then only a few months after the Second Battle of Ypres and the first gas attack. They were all full of ideas about frightfulness. I'm glad I didn't go in for that. At one time I wanted to – I thought it was a new departure and might develop.

Well, we were all thoroughly bored with the depot [at Rouen] and spent most of our time down in the town, getting back about eleven in the evening. There was nothing to do in the town except eat and spend money generally.

On the 5th August, the first of us were called away. There were curious things called entrenching battalions[13] being formed just then and Panet went to one of them with twenty sappers. We were all very alarmed and disconcerted. Entrenching battalions. What were they? Where are we all going to spend our days in solitary state, attached to scratch infantry battalions, digging trenches miles behind the line? I went to the DAG's[14] office to try and get them to send me to a field company. It was no good. Appointments were done from GHQ[15] apparently.

Two days later four more of us went off, including Grindley, all to different entrenching battalions.

11th August 1915

On Wednesday, 11th August, I also left with twenty sappers for No. 10 EB.[16] We marched down to the station at 1.30 pm and had to wait until 5.30 pm before the train went. I saw my little party into the train, complete with rations, and went to get something to eat at the countess of somebody's tea stall.

It was a miserable journey. I was dressed like a Christmas tree[17] with water bottle and mess tin etc. but I hadn't got anything to read. I had a rotten feeling the whole time that I hadn't thought of anything, that I might have been quite comfortable if only I'd brought the right things with me.

The train of course was continually stopping, and people were getting out to pick flowers or to get hot water from the engine. I felt awfully responsible. They formed my first little command, those twenty Sappers.

We got to Poperinghe[18] about 3.30 pm the next day. There was no one there who knew anything about the 10th Entrenching Battalion. However, after a lot of telephoning, the RTO managed to get on to someone who did, and a guide was to be sent for me. We would have to wait.

So, this was Poperinghe. There was a Bosch[19] aeroplane over the town when we arrived and they were shooting at it.

I still had a very vague idea of the line or where it was. I had no map. I knew we were somewhere a few miles behind Ypres. I had been told they shelled Poperinghe, so it seemed to be more or less in the war zone. There were very few people around that afternoon. I wandered down into the square and got some tea. There were several aeroplanes about. I didn't know in the least whether they were ours or not. It was all very interesting and novel. The shops all had Flemish names.

The guide arrived at about 5.30 pm in the evening and we marched up through the square and out along the Westvleteren Road.

It was very hot and dusty. There were more aeroplanes over. I wondered what one did if a Bosch came over. We had been told that we ought to take cover and that the Bosch oughtn't to be allowed to see troops moving. But how was one to know if they were Bosch or not? With one's field glasses I supposed. I wondered how long it would take to get to know about things.

There were fields all along, and the dirty little estaminets[20] with unpronounceable names. I heard several guns going off, but I didn't notice them much.

We marched along that road for about 2 miles and then turned off to the left into Hamoek Woods. I was shown one or two tents far into the wood. The Battalion apparently hadn't arrived. I was taken off to see 'headquarters', which consisted of a colonel, an adjutant, and a doctor. They lived in tents and seemed very comfortable in them. I had a good tea there. Apparently, this was the headquarters of a kind of group of entrenching battalions, only one of which had as yet arrived. We were going to dig a line of trenches somewhere.

I went back to what was to become the battalion camp. The section had got a fire going and were making themselves comfortable. The wood was typical of every wood, from Poperinghe northwards. Young oaks with an undergrowth of hazel. It was damp and steamy in spite of the heat of the weather. Dotted about there were curious mounds about 40 feet across and 10 high, surrounded by a kind of shallow moat containing peaty mud and rushes and water. The soil was all yellow clay with a very thin covering of moss and roots. Those woods were always damp and steamy and rather depressing. The oaks were very thick overhead, so little sunlight got in. The tents were dotted about wherever they could fit in between the trees. People were evidently very nervous of being seen by aeroplanes.

Late that night the battalion arrived. Someone stumbled into my tent and asked who the devil I was. There was a great noise and fuss while they were settling down. Eventually three officers came in to share my tent.

In the morning there was a general arranging and tidying up of things. The three fellows in my tent belonged to B Company, and it was arranged that I should mess with B Company. They were an awfully nice lot of fellows. All Irishmen. The battalion was set to work to make bivouacs for themselves. I had a few specimens made for them to copy. We made them all out of the brushwood that grew about.

The battalion was a motley collection. There was something like forty-five different regiments represented. It was a kind of advanced reinforcement camp organised as a battalion for labour. Drafts would be sent out from it to the various infantry battalions in the army.

On the 14th [August], we started work. We paraded at 7.00 am and marched about four miles to Steentje Mill on the Poperinghe–Elverdinghe road. It was scorching hot. Here we were met by sappers of the 7th Field Company, who led each party away to their work. My sappers were distributed among the field company men, chiefly, I suppose, to learn the job. There was nothing really for me to do except to do the same: learn things.

The 7th Field Company was constructing a series of four defensive posts,[21] forming part of a general line, running through St Sixte and Steentje Mill and joining up with the existing GHQ line running south from just behind Vlamertinghe. These were large posts of about 500 yards across and were intended for all-round defence. Each of them was sited in a wood and consisted of small earthworks, all above ground (because of the water in winter) to hold a platoon each. The small elements were afterwards to be connected to form a complete fort to hold about a battalion. The scheme had been started about a fortnight before we arrived.

Our battalion was to work with No. 1 Section of the company. They were working on a post in the woods, just south of Steentje Mill. The RE officer in charge was Ashcroft whom I had met at Chatham. He was a Canadian from Kingston[22] College and didn't mind talking about his job. I learnt a lot from him.

I wandered around by myself most of that morning. I watched how the field company men were showing the new infantry how to lay sandbags and how to dig. I watched the big parapets growing, the earth being got from 'borrow pits' in front. They had to dig it away as best they could from around the roots of the hazel brushwood growing everywhere. Everything was so new and fresh and interesting. You could hear the guns very loud when they fired, but they were very quiet that day. I liked the smell of the new earth as it was thrown up. It was a cloudless day, hot and dusty. I still wore more or less of a Christmas tree and didn't understand things a bit. I didn't know what one should take out with one for these jobs. I had been provided with field glasses[23] before I came out from England, and I suppose they were wanted, so I wore them. What for I couldn't tell. There was a great craze for staring at aeroplanes and trying to discover if they were ours or not. Everyone was frightened of being seen. That was the only use I could see for field glasses. I also wore web equipment, and a haversack and water bottle, not because I thought I should want it, but because I had been provided with it, and it must be some use. I regarded life still as a kind of parade.

Several times I went to the eastern edge of the wood and look out towards the line. You could see quite a distance. I borrowed a map from Ashcroft: Sheet 28 it must have been. I must have seen Elverdinghe Wood and Woesten. I didn't know at all where the line was. Even that first morning I had a feeling that this perhaps wasn't really right in the war. The line must still be some way away. An incomprehensible thing. It was a very still day and you could hear the occasional rifle shots.

The men knocked off work at about 12.30 pm for lunch, which they brought with them. They made tea in dixies. I found the officers who shared my tent, and we went in search of something to eat. Ashcroft had indicated an estaminet somewhere nearby.

We got good omelettes there in a little kind of summer house made of withies.[24] The place was the Viulle Seule Cabaret it is marked on the map at A24, B83. Translated, it means 'dirty bucket cabaret'. I think this was about the edge of civilian life then. The crops and hop fields grew up to about this point, and then fell away towards the east into grassland, trees and untilled fields. There were probably a few isolated people living in tumbledown cottages further forward and to the left they seemed to live nearer up.[25]

We knocked off at about 4.30 pm and marched back to camp. The woods were nice and cool when we got there and we had tea and rested and talked and generally got to know one another. The guns were going occasionally. You could hear them rolling and echoing through the wood. It was a wonderful place for sound that wood. The guns were at least 4 miles in front. As it got dark, you could even hear the rifle fire from the Front quite distinctly. About 7.30 pm there was a bigger bang than usual, that echoed in an extraordinary way. About ten seconds later there was a faint noise which gradually increased to a long, drawn-out whistle, like someone whistling rather badly and letting out an unnecessary amount of air: the first shell we'd heard. It seemed to come out of the sky from another world and it died away to the south of Poperinghe. The peculiar pathetic sound of a very long-range shell.

That night as I was going to bed, I dug out a root which was likely to be uncomfortable under my valise. It was dark in the tent and the root glowed all over quite brightly. We dug up some more roots and they all glowed. I went to sleep thinking of everything I'd seen. I could see queer lights through the tent flap and through the trees to the east. They grew and flickered and died down. The guns popped off from time to time singly, and each one echoed: that drawn-out rolling echo of the shell going over the woods. Little spatters of rifle fire came intermittently from far away. What queer country it was, these damp woods of luxuriant and young oaks. Everything was so rank and luxuriant, even the roots glowed. The crops we had passed on the road were heavier that I had ever seen. There was a field of maize quite 7 feet high. The land was not flat; there were several ups and downs, and yet the ground was damp, although it hadn't rained for weeks. The ditches that ran through the woods everywhere all wet at the bottom.

The other fellows in the tent were asleep. It was the first time I had ever been right away from people I knew. We were all perfect strangers, and yet we all lived together and chatted as if we had known each other for weeks. There was Casey who had just left Sandhurst, and Captain Long of the Dublin Fusiliers. Both of them had only just come out for the first time. I wondered what they thought of things.

The same thing happened next morning, and every day afterwards. We marched up to Steentje Mill, and the work went on. Ashcroft would come round and give instructions and see that the infantry were working. His corporal carried on when he wasn't there. Ashcroft would take me around and show me how to lay sandbags, and how to revet[26] the sides of trenches with wire netting and stakes tied back at the top, with binding wire to pickets.[27] He told me all about laying out trenches in the line, and what kind of trenches were made. He didn't say anything about the line in front of us. He hadn't been up there. He was in the line at Kemmel, before the company came back to do this job.

19th August 1915 [approximately]

Ashcroft took me round to the 57th Field Company for breakfast. Their billets were just on the edge of the wood where the work was going on. They belong to the 49th Division who were holding the line in front. There were several people that I knew from Chatham and from the Shop.

Up until now I hadn't thought much about who was holding the actual line in front of us. One never seemed to see troops on the road. In my mind, the line was still far away, an unapproachable, mysterious thing to which troops went. A place where men fired rifles at night and lights came from star shells that shot up in the air at night and burst into brilliant white light.

For the first time I was meeting men who really belonged to the Front and who spent most of the time there. I suddenly realised how detached we were from the real life at the Front. We weren't at the Front at all. They had a black tarred hut for a mess. It seemed to be the only hut there was. They lived in tents and dugouts of corrugated iron and sandbags. Their horse lines were all round in the wood.

There were two subalterns in the mess when we got there. One was having breakfast, and the other was having dinner before going to bed. The others were in bed. Maclean was talking about the job he had just come back from. He'd had several sappers wounded. The talk was all about a bridge over a canal that they were building at night. Ashcroft had said something about the canal. They were a very cheery lot. Maclean was ragging with Ashcroft and they upset the table.

I wondered what kind of job it was they were doing up there. The line and the canal were a mystery and a romance and remained so.

That afternoon, without any warning, there was a great swish, just over my head it seemed; an angry, mechanical noise, almost a screech, as if it was coming straight at one. The shell burst about 20 yards behind me and produced a whining sound which rapidly died away as the shrapnel bullets struck things and stopped. We crouched involuntarily against the new parapet and waited in silence for a moment, expecting another. The RE corporal was hit in the throat and cheek and Ashcroft was busy bandaging him. Several more shells were put over before we left but no further harm was done.

Nothing particular happened for several weeks after that. Some days I went out to work but there was nothing to do. Other days I did odd jobs about the camp. Water got very short and I had to dig shallow wells in the clay. In the evenings, we strolled over to St Sixte to buy eggs and things or went down Poperinghe. Poperinghe was then the social centre of about half the army. It was then hardly knocked about at all. True they shelled it nearly every day, but most of the shells were duds and the hits were mostly in behind the houses and didn't show. One could buy almost anything there. The reserve brigades[28] of all the divisions in the Salient lived round about and came in in the evening.

It was a wonderful place Poperinghe. There was an air of subdued festivity. Things in the Salient were about as bad as they could be. The fighting at Hooge had been going on for months with only a lull for a week or so. People came into Poperinghe to buy food for their messes and to have a bit of a dinner at Ginger's. The 6th Division 'Fancies'[29] had posters about the place. 'A Hooge Success' etc. I think the civilians still remembered the Second Battle [of Ypres] and the gas; they still looked on the British as their defenders to a certain extent and weren't simply out to make money as they were afterwards.

I remember how surprised I was sat there being anything like that the Fancies going on in a place like Poperinghe. The hall where they played had a slight hole through the roof of it.

There was a wonderful atmosphere of romance about the place specially on coming out of the Fancies on a dark evening and seeing the great gun flashes and the flickering Verey lights in the sky. Afterwards you went round into the square towards Ginger's Restaurant [tea shop], and you heard people talking about Ypres and the Menin Road, and of the canal and the Dead End.

One night, about the second week in September, I went up to Elverdinghe with the quartermaster to get some waggon loads of bricks to make horse standings. The village had just been condemned by the CRE[30] 49th Division as being uninhabitable, and so was open by night to any unit that wanted to get bricks for their horse lines etc. Elverdinghe was about 1.5 miles behind the line; much nearer to it than any of us had been before. Sometimes we had seen shells bursting there, or rather, we had seen the pink brick dust rise above the treetops of Elverdinghe Wood in the daytime while we were working near Steentje Mill.

We started at seven o'clock with four wagons and trekked up the Woesten Road to De Wippe Cabaret and then, down to the right on to the Poperinghe–Elverdinghe road and up to the outskirts of the village. It took about an hour and a quarter and it was quite dark when we got there. We passed a lot of French on the road with guns and wagons etc. They were holding the line on the left of the 49th Division apparently, and Elverdinghe was on the boundary line between them.

I was struck by the streams of transport on the roads everywhere. So, this was when everything got done. I hadn't realised how nocturnal the war was. In the daytime the roads were all empty and one hardly ever saw a wagon or a lorry.

By the time we got to the village the moon was out. We were stopped just outside and had to wait in a long column. They [the Germans] were shelling the village. This was going to be exciting. We could see the roofs of the houses sticking up in the moonlight like skeletons. There were very few tiles left. After a bit we moved on and pulled up at the side of the road by a likely house that had a lot of loose bricks about. The men began to load up, and Attoe and I went along to explore. The Bosch had apparently only quite recently turned their serious attention to Elverdinghe. A great many of all the houses were in good condition, except that most of the roofs were off. At the south-eastern end near the church, the damage was much greater. Several of the houses were mere heaps of bricks, and of the church itself nothing much remained except the tower, which stood up in the moonlight against the dark background of the wood, a white broken thing. The graveyard had been more or less torn up by shells and there was a faint smell like stale cheese that I didn't know the meaning of then. The whole place had that unforgettable smell of fresh ruins: a dry smell of accumulated household dirt suddenly exposed to the air, and of brick dust.

In between the rattle of horse transport on the paved road there were short intervals of dead silence. Then a machine gun would start over to the east where the line was. It seemed quite loud and close now and broke the silence with a clear, sharp, strident noise. You could feel the silence in between each burst of fire.

We went round to see if there was anything useful in the place. It was great fun groping around in the rooms and cellars. It wasn't really looting, for the houses would all be knocked down soon and there was no harm in getting what one could. How flimsy and sordid human dwelling really are when the furniture is broken up, and the walls are down so that you can see into the rooms. And the smell: all houses smell the same when they are disturbed. It doesn't matter who the occupants were.

The spirit of romance was very strong that night. The war was very much closer to us than it had been before. We were almost in front of the guns: a howitzer would 'poop' off in Elverdinghe Wood with a great yellow flash now and again and the French 75s would fire salvos from somewhere behind. What a lot we would be able to tell the others back at the camp.

I went up to Elverdinghe most nights after that. We brought back bricks for the stables and also beds and tables for ourselves. Every night the place changed. More and more houses were knocked down. They must have shelled it badly every day. One night we brought back a dud shell in one of the wagons, right on top of the stones (what fools we were). We put it outside the Adjutant's tent as if it had fallen there in the night.

On the evening of 24th September, we could hear a heavy bombardment going on somewhere. The whole ground and air seemed to be vibrating to it. What was it? What was happening over there to the south-east? As it grew dark we could see the sky flickering continuously like one long flash of summer lightning. I woke up several times in the night and it was going on still. The whole country seemed to be trembling.

The 25th September was very wet. It rained nearly all day. The bombardment was still going on. In the afternoon it was reported that there were streams of ambulances going through Poperinghe and there were all sorts of wild rumours of battles and attacks.

Next morning, we heard of the great advance of 3 miles at Loos and of the capture of 10,000 prisoners. Of the big attack at Hooge we heard nothing. One never does hear of failures until long afterwards. It was the dud attack at Hooge that we had heard on the previous night, not the 'great advance' at Loos.

30th September 1915

On Monday, everybody was ordered away. Reinforcements were wanted in practically every regiment represented in the battalion. Next day, I got my orders too and very glad I was to get them. I had been getting more and more bored and was beginning to think I was going to stay there indefinitely. However, here were my orders. To proceed to join the 83rd Field Company, 20th Division forthwith. At last I was going to belong to a field company like Ashcroft, Maclean and the others and to do real things 'in the line'.

I'm afraid that all this has been a monstrous and disjointed account of dull and uninteresting events, but everything seemed very thrilling and full of new sensations and impressions. I took away with me a strange fascination for that weird, misty country: its damp, dripping oak woods with their echoes of distant firing, its hop fields and rank maize plots and its inhabitants with their strange language. They seem to be a forgotten people, living in a remote and neglected country on the outskirts of civilization.

By a series of curious coincidences, I returned to that country in different capacities many times. My fascination with it increased rather than diminished with each visit.

MAPS

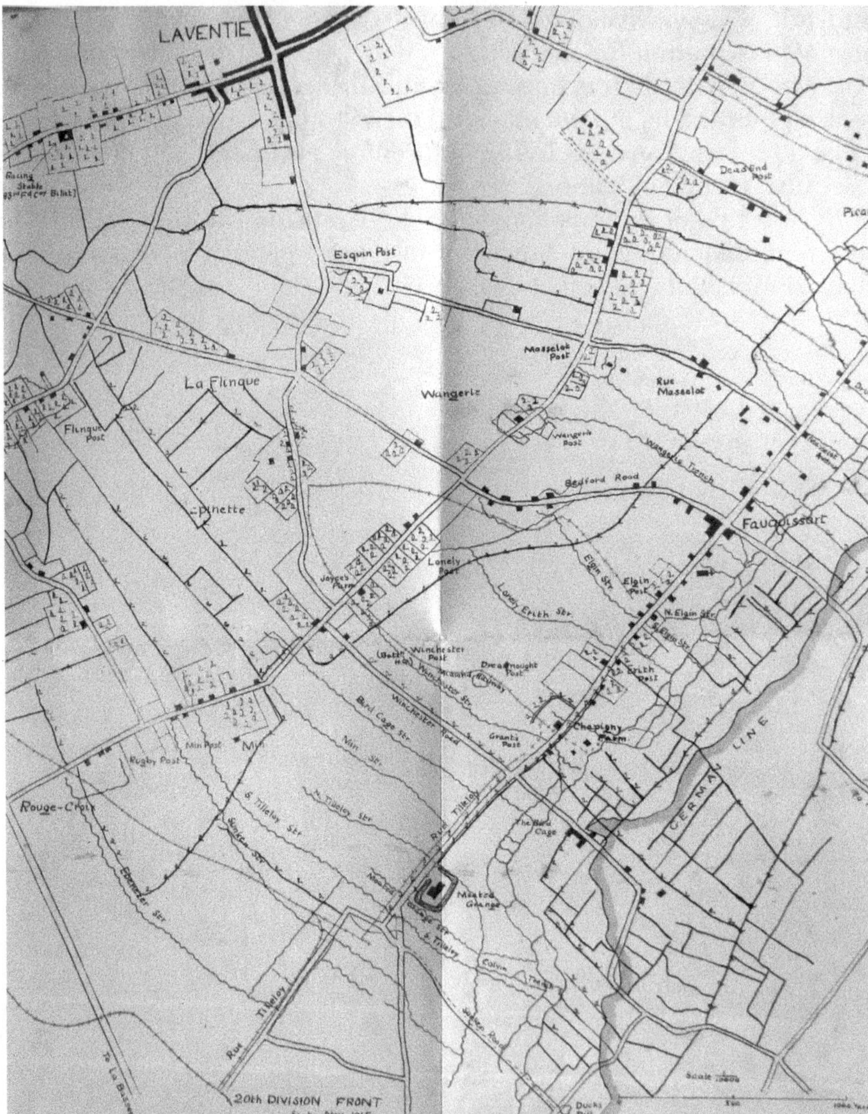

Laventie, September to November 1915. Bagnold Family Archive.

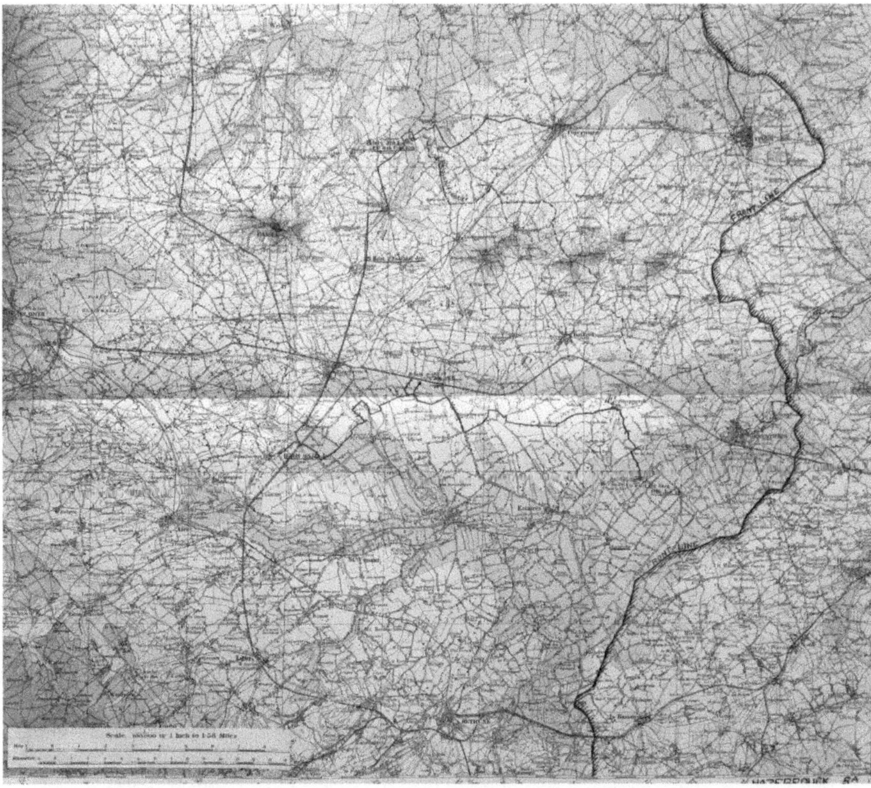

Journey from Laventie to Ypres, 11th to 31st January 1916. Bagnold Family Archive.

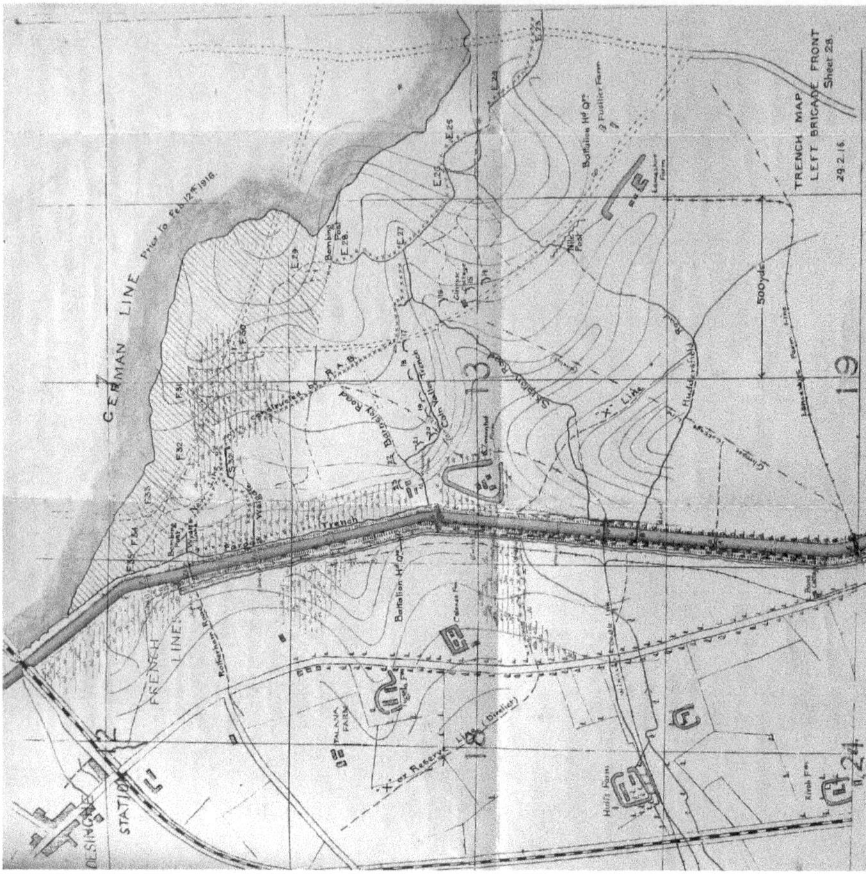

Yser Canal, 12th to 29th February 1916. Bagnold Family Archive.

60th Brigade Front, Ypres, May to July 1916. Bagnold Family Archive.

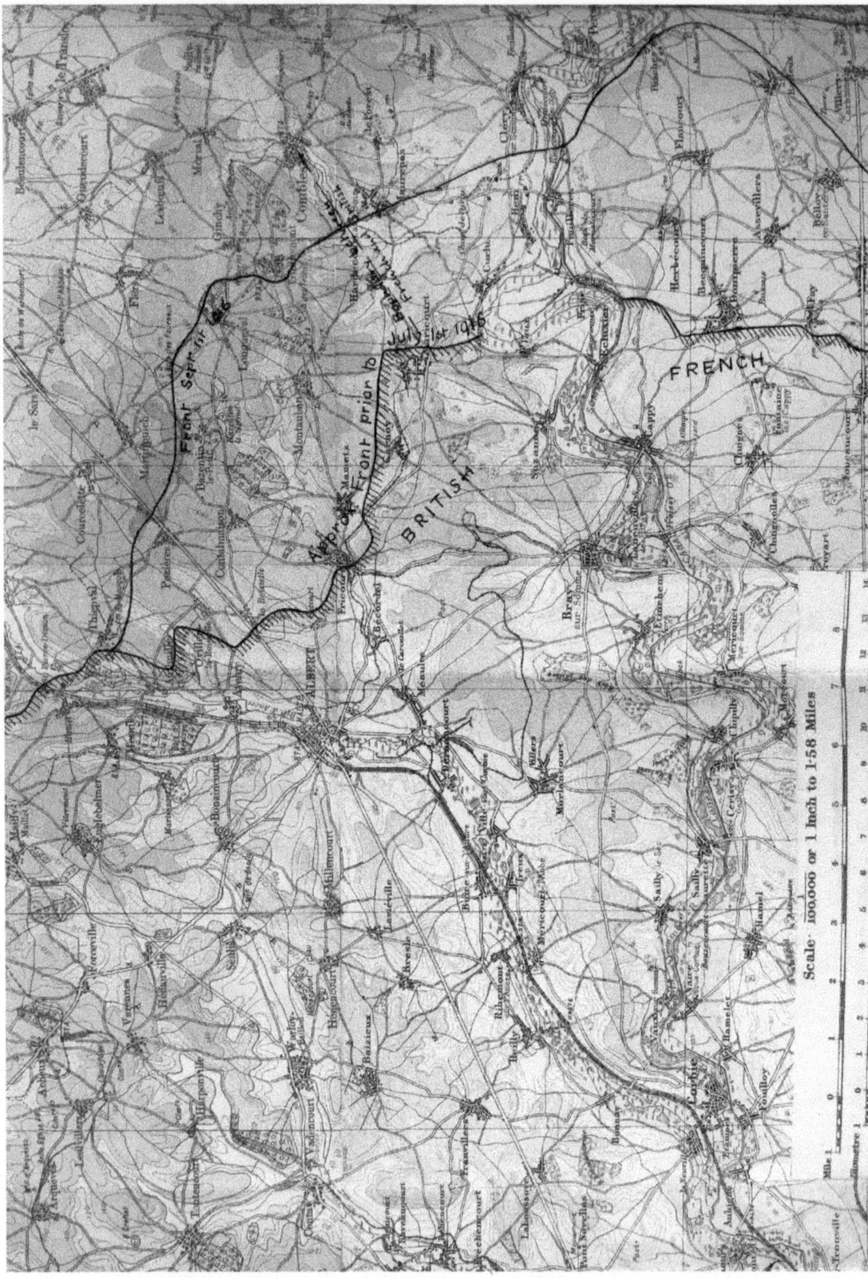

Somme Sector, East of Albert, 1st July to 1st September 1916. Bagnold Family Archive.

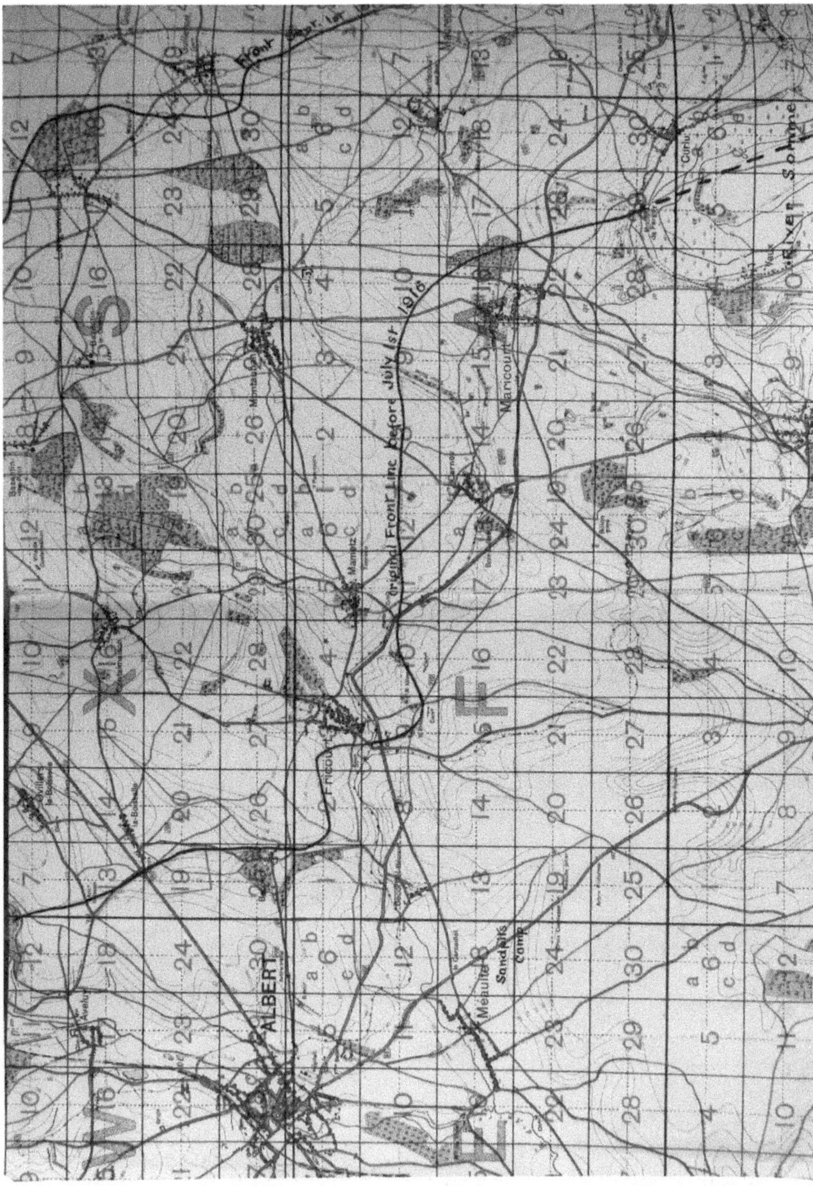

Somme Sector, Detail, 1st July to 1st September 1916. Bagnold Family Archive.

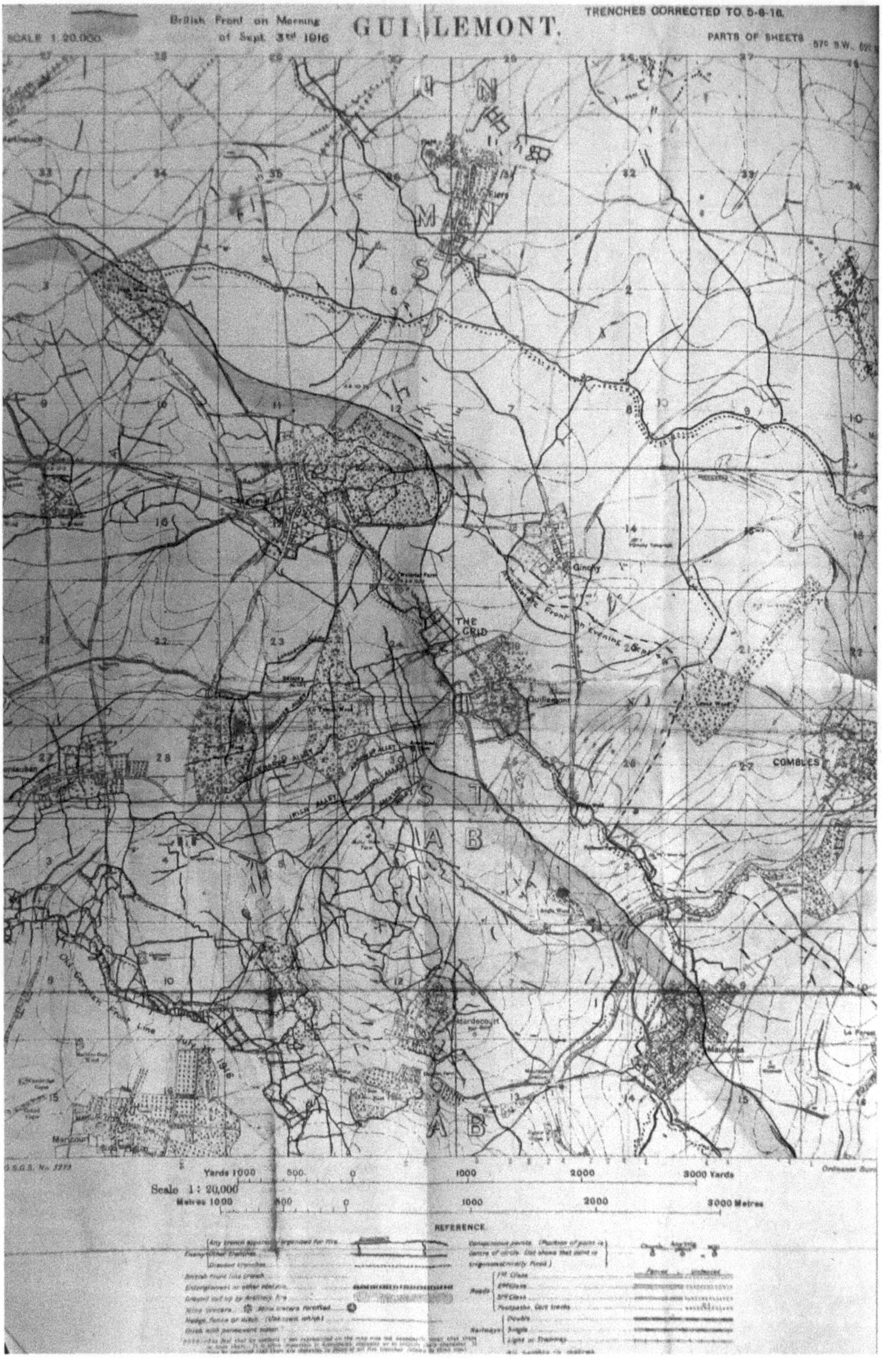

Map of Guillemont showing approximate position of front line on 4th September 1916. Bagnold Family Archive.

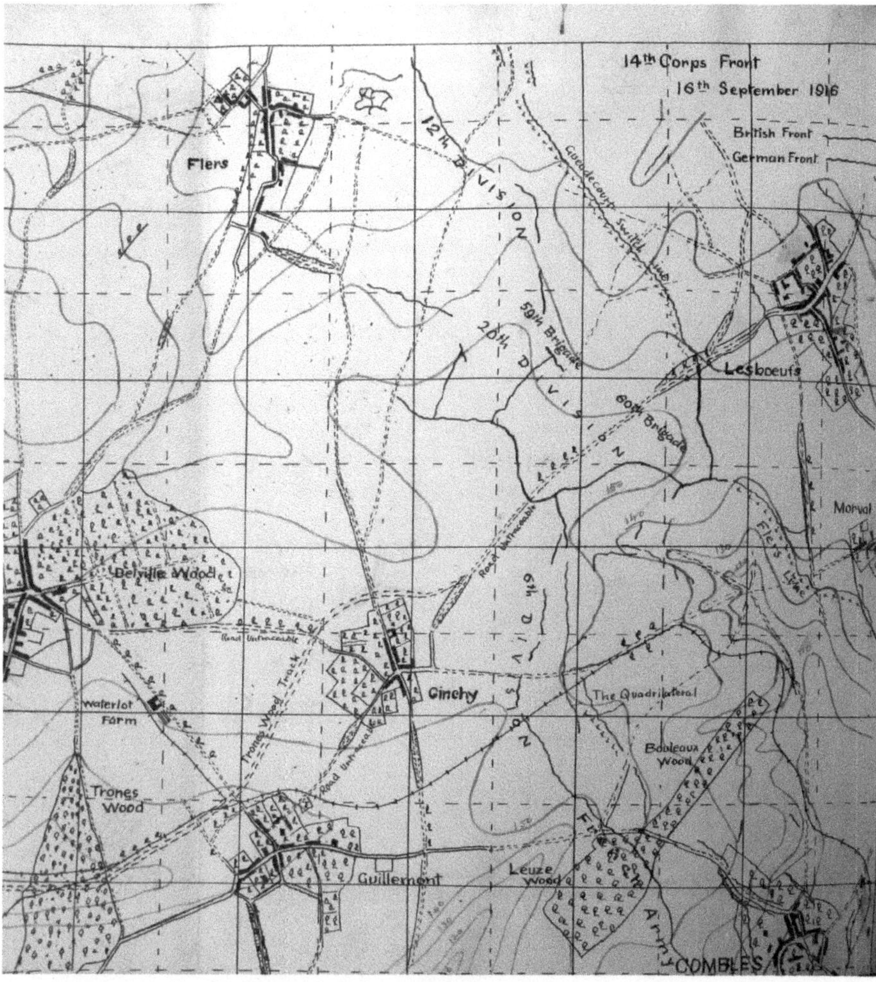

14th Corps Front near Flers and Ginchy, 16th September 1916. Bagnold Family Archive.

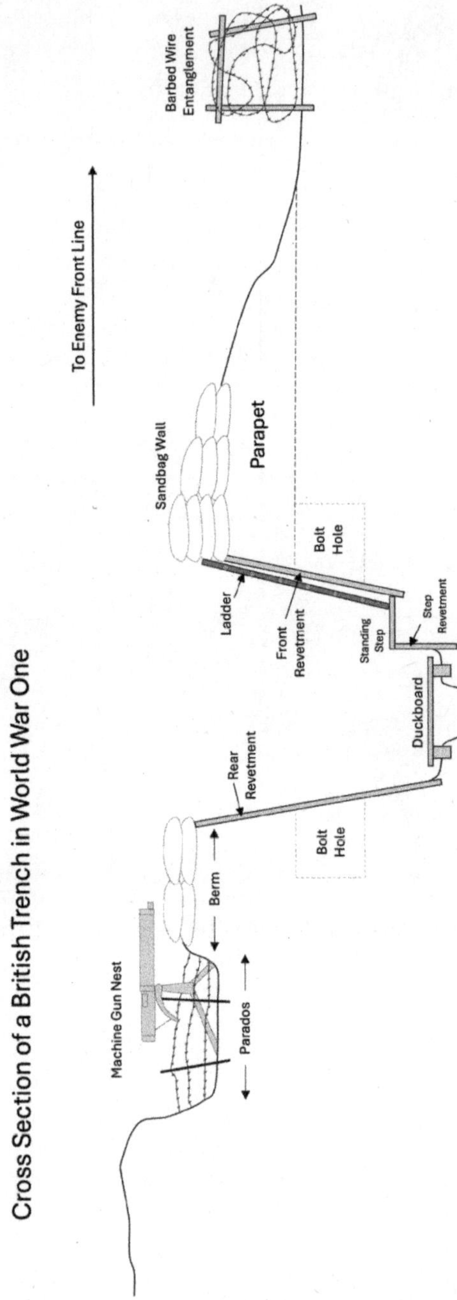

Cross-section of a First World War trench (drawn by Christopher Bagnold). Bagnold Family Archive.

Chapter 1

THE 83rd FIELD COMPANY (OCTOBER 1915–JANUARY 1916)

Laventie

I have been wondering how to go on. I should have liked to have written a kind of history of the company, but I don't think this is possible. No, it will have to be a story from my own point of view, illustrated with my own impressions. I joined the company as a reinforcement, while the others had come out [to France] with it, so naturally their impressions and their points of view were different from mine, at any rate for the first months. At the beginning I was only interested in my own little jobs and didn't take much interest in what the other sections were doing. However, we were all in the same company and we did the same work and lived together so I suppose we must have seen things in more or less the same light.

1st October 1915

Well, after much travelling, I arrived at La Gorge station and was directed to the CRE's office. It happened to be the office of the CRE of the wrong division. I think it must have been the Meerut Division. But with the guidance of an Indian orderly, I eventually found the 20th Division HQ[31] in the adjoining town of Estaires and arrived in time for lunch at the CRE's mess. The CRE was out but I had something to eat with the Adjutant, Massey and the divisional RE doctor, one Leckey.

I asked them a lot of questions about the 83rd Field Company. Massey was very vague. I asked what sort of man the OC[32] was and Massey looked enquiringly at Leckey and said he thought he was a good chap. Yes, he supposed Hopkins was a good OC.

They were all having tea when I arrived at the company billet at Laventie. I think it was Scott who met me first and introduced me.

They had asked a few questions about my journey but mostly they left me to myself. I suppose I must have been an object of considerable interest. I was their first reinforcement officer.

The 20th Division had been in the line about a month and a half. Curiously enough they had landed in France only a day after I had. They had been sent by train from Havre to St Omer and marched up from there in gradual stages. At first, they had been introduced to the line a brigade at a time and had been attached to the 8th Division for instruction. The latter were then holding the line from about La Cordonnerie Farm to just south of Champigny Farm.

It was about the first week in September that the 20th Division was considered fully fledged and were given a piece of the line to hold by themselves. It was the right half of the 8th Division front and stretched from Picantin to Winchester Road.

From now on, there were rumours of a big attack coming off. In a few days, preparations began to be made. There were dugouts to be built, more communication trenches to be made, assembly trenches to be dug and dumps of material and stores to be collected. What excitement there must have been as the great day came on. There was going to be a great advance and the Aubers Ridge was going to be captured. The whole thing was to be in conjunction with the main attack north of Lens ('The Offensive at Loos'). Kits were all packed up ready and wagons and bridging material overhauled. The dismal attack on Fromelles by the 8th Division earlier in the year and the skeletons still lying out there beyond the front line were all forgotten.

I could never quite gather the actual details of what precisely did happen on 25th September on the Laventie front. It was another so-called 'holding attack' like the one at Hooge. It was the old story. They went over full of dash and enthusiasm; there wasn't much opposition apparently. Then came a counterattack; someone on the right began to fall back; there were no reinforcements whatever and the whole lot had to come back to their original line. The Indians on the right lost very heavily. The company itself had quite a few casualties, including one officer Haycroft, the senior subaltern and OC No. 1 Section. He had been hit in the thigh with a bullet and had gone to the base.

The talk that afternoon was chiefly about 25th September and about Haycroft.

***

After tea, Hopkins asked me a lot of questions about what I'd been taught at Chatham and how long I'd been there etc. He told me I was to take over Haycroft's section, which Captain Scott, the second in command, was looking after temporarily.

For a very long time I couldn't understand the major. I don't think the others did either. He was a regular sapper of about fifteen years' service, most of which I believe he had spent in India. He was a tall man about 6 feet 2 [inches] with faded red hair, and a rather hooked nose and a red, sunburned face. He was the bluntest, most short-spoken man I have ever met, and he gave me the impression of having a terrible temper, which he was unsuccessfully, but with great effort, keeping under control. This wasn't really the case, although he did have a bad liver in the mornings. He had a most disconcerting habit, especially with strangers, of not answering a question. No one liked to ask a second time. You got the impression that he had certainly heard, but didn't think your remark worth answering. He would sit at the end of the table in the mess and say nothing, except occasionally grumble at the food. Sometimes he would make a remark: it was sure to be an unusual kind of remark, very short and to the point and often with a dry cynical humour. Sometimes he would give a guffaw of laughter very suddenly at something someone had said. He liked to hear one make a cynical remark especially about someone he didn't like. It was one of the few occasions at which he'd relax: he'd sniff and smile sardonically like a great red-haired hawk.

Friends he had very few that we could discover. Apart from ourselves, his juniors were also frightened of him, and the battalion commanders and others senior to him disliked him chiefly because of his unfortunate manner.

***

The evening I arrived, Scott took me up towards the line to show me what my future section was doing and to see about laying rails for a new bit of tramway.

The 60th Brigade, to which our company was attached, had side-stepped to the right three days before, only retaining about 800 yards of the bit of the front line that they had held before. Each of the four sections of the field company had a quarter of the brigade front to look after and luckily my bit was the old bit that the company had been working on for several weeks. The others had areas that had just been taken over from a brigade of the Meerut Division and all the trenches were in a very bad state. The brigade front now stretched from Champigny Farm on the left or north, down to the Duck's Bill, a curious little salient jutting out into no man's land a few hundred yards north of Neuve Chapelle.

We walked up from the company billet in the Rue Paradis just outside Laventie along the road past La Flinque crossroads to L'Epiniette Farm. Here a little tramway started, which ran up to the line 2,000 yards away.

The country as far as La Flinque was still cultivated. I suppose this was one of the quietest bits of the Front in those days. Along the roads there were high, overgrown hedges and every 200 yards or so a farm with a little orchard and a clump of trees round it. Around every field there were great deep ditches running into large hollows at the corners. The land was rather like a flat spring cushion, the fields rising slightly towards the centre from the ditches at the sides. For this reason, one didn't notice that the country was really dead level.

As we walked on, Scott told me about the events of the last week and about the work that was going on now. I liked Scott from the first. He was one of those large, plump people who always seemed contented and satisfied with life.

He was a regular sapper like Hopkins and was full of stories and anecdotes about India and racing. If Hopkins was silent and taciturn, Scott made up for it with his cheeriness and good temper. He was one of those men who seem to have nothing whatever to do and yet got through more than most people. He was always the last down to breakfast in the morning and last to leave the mess at night.

Normally the second-in-command's job in a field company is to look after the stores and rations, the headquarters transport and, when the company was in the line, the section transport as well. He was responsible for the workshops and for the delivery of all RE stores to the brigade and battalions, and to the four sections of the company.

From Epinette we walked along the wooden tramway to where it crossed the Rue Bacqueret. Here there were sidings and piles of RE material such as timber, planking, and 9- by 3-inch joists, corrugated iron, barbed wire, pickets, picks and shovels by the hundred. It was my section dump. Corporal Joyce lived there and presided over it. In the farm ('Joyce's Farm') there were more tools, chiefly carpenters' tools belonging to the section, which were used daily and kept there to save taking them back to the tool cart. There were also explosives, boxes of guncotton and detonators, cable and exploders.

We went in to see Joyce. The place was full of rats and was half tumbled down. In one corner there was a kind of dugout affair which the storekeepers had made for themselves in case the farm was shelled.

It was getting a bit dark now and the evening traffic on the railway was just beginning. Trucks loaded with rations and water for the men in the front line were being pushed up from Epinette. More trucks and carrying parties of infantry were waiting at Joyce's Farm for corrugated iron or timber to be issued to them.

Scott having settled the business of stores with Joyce, we went along the track through the orchard and out into the open fields of long, uncut autumn hay.

It was very slippery. Along both sides of the track and in the middle between the rails the grassland had been worn away, leaving the greasy yellow clay. Now and then we had to get off the long grass and thistles to make way for the ration trucks. Several times we passed a party in distress with their truck off the rails and the wheels deep in the mud. Scott said the wooden rails weren't at all satisfactory, but there wasn't anything else.

Presently a faint flickering far away to the left showed where the first star shell of the evening had been fired. Dusk was coming on, and first one light and then another fluttered up from behind the screen of hedges and trees to the right and left, hovering in the air and then falling, going out as it fell. Straight ahead of us a bright one shot up suddenly, throwing a ruined farm and some poplars into swaying silhouette. The front line must only be a few hundred yards away. This was the edge of the strange nocturnal land of the Front that we had seen from a distance and wondered about, away up in the damp oak woods north of Poperinghe.

Up to now things had been very quiet; the desultory rifle shooting however was gradually increasing as darkness came on. Suddenly there was a *'rat-tat-tat-tat'* from somewhere in front followed immediately by a series of little swishes that seemed in a hurry to catch up with one another. In a second or two they got much louder and Scott dropped to the ground like a stone. I did the same because he did. Then I could hear bullets striking the ground a few yards behind us. It lasted only a moment or so, and then Scott got up and went on as if nothing had happened. Shortly afterwards there was a 'Wheew' just over our heads. Involuntarily I ducked and at the same time noticed Scott hadn't. Apparently, it wasn't done to duck. I mustn't do it again. After that there was quite a lot of seemingly aimless rifle fire.

I think I preserved quite an open mind about it all. I certainly wasn't a bit frightened. It was all so wonderfully novel and interesting. If other people treated bullets swishing by them as a matter of course, it must be all right. Anyhow, if one was hit, why, it couldn't be helped. At that

I left it. All the same it was hard to prevent oneself from ducking when a bullet came near.

At Champigny, or Chaplin Farm as it was called, the tramway ended. The trucks were being off-loaded and the contents carried off up a trench to the accompaniment of a good deal of swearing and cries of 'Who the ******* hell lit that cigarette?' or 'Put that ******* cigarette out'.

It was still light enough to see things. There were two jobs to be prospected for. The railway had to be continued on to the front line, 200 yards further on and a branch was to be made bending to the right and running along Rue Tilleroy to join up with the tramway in Schon's sector on the right. The branch was to be done first, so we selected the best line for it and pegged it out roughly. It was too dark though, and we decided to go back.

I shared a room with Lieutenant[33] Jervis in the company billet at Laventie. He was a Scotchman, about twenty-seven, rather small and sharp-featured and he spoke in the quick, clipped way of Glasgow. A year ago, he had been an electrical engineer.

We talked about lots of things that night. About the other officers in the company, about my section and what they had done on the day of the battle a week ago, and about Major Hopkins and his way of disconcerting people. I gathered he wasn't liked in the brigade. 'Old Roy', the brigadier had his knife into him and the battalion commanders didn't care for him either:

> But it's only his way, he takes a lot of knowing. D'ye know what he said about you when you'd gone out after tea? He sat there for a long time and puffed away with his old pipe and then he said quite suddenly, 'He beats you all for boots anyway'.

Next morning, each section paraded separately outside their billets and were detailed for their various jobs. Some were employed in the workshops making trench-boards etc. The painters were mostly doing noticeboards with the names of the various trenches in the line. The remainder marched off up to the Front to help the infantry with the dugouts etc.

The company billet was a very large racing stable in Rue Paradis about 200 yards from the crossroads in Laventie. It was under 2 miles from the line. It seems hardly creditable now, but it was absolutely intact and no shells had ever come near it. The house itself had all modern conveniences including a bath with hot and cold water laid on. We only used a part of the house, the rest of which was occupied by half the reserve battalion of the brigade. Two companies would come and live there for a week and then be relieved by some other battalion.

Our mess looked out on to a little court with a garden in the centre of it. The men were billeted in the barns on the farther side. Leading off from this court was another much larger yard, connected to it by an archway. The whole of this second yard was surrounded by stables in which were accommodated our eighty-odd horses and mules and also our workshops. Above, lived our drivers and the infantry. In the centre was a midden[34] and round it were piled our stores.

That morning I went up the line with Scott and Schon. We went on bicycles. The roads were very muddy and I had a hard job to keep up with the others as I hadn't ridden a bicycle for a long time. It looked as if bicycles were the usual way of getting about.

At Chaplin Farm there was a small, advanced store,[35] from which Schon extracted tape and pickets. He had done a lot of surveying for the CPR[36] in Canada just before the war and therefore took charge of the laying out of the curves for the tramway so as to avoid as many obstacles – such as trees and the remains of houses – as possible. Schon was one of those fat genial people who delight in the unconventional.

This railway job pleased me like anything. It was like the model railway I used to play with at home only more interesting. There were points and crossings to be made, special ones to be designed that could be constructed from wood. There were bridges to be built over trenches and obstacles such as house walls to be blown up or cut through. Above all there was the thrill attached to the proximity to the line, the idea that at last I was really part of the actual machinery of the war.

The front line at Laventie was a most uninteresting place – at any rate by day. Except for an occasional rifle shot, there mightn't have been a war on at all. Scott took me up that afternoon. We went to a communication trench into which I had seen the ration party disappear the evening before. It was a very good trench then, nearly dry. It seemed to be full of little frogs. The yellow clay sides were covered with a thin green fungus where the sun couldn't get to them. There were telephone cables everywhere, crossing the trench at every corner. Some were just about neck high, laid along the top of the trench, others were all across the bottom and got tangled in one's feet.

The front line then consisted of a rough irregular breastwork, about 3 or 4 feet high above the ground, behind which there was a shallow trench a foot or so deep. Everything seemed to be made of decaying sandbags, only prevented from collapsing by occasional light wooden revetting[37] frames, tied back through the parapet by insufficient wire. In most places there was just the parapet, the gangway behind, and nothing else. Here and there behind the gangway were crazy shelters[38] half in the ground and half above. They were just little mounds of earth with a hole of scooped out at the side, covered by an insufficiently supported sheet of corrugated iron. There was just room to crawl in and lie down.

The whole place smelt of decaying food and stale humanity. There were tins lying about everywhere trodden into the mud.

There seemed to be no one about; just an occasional sentry looking through a periscope and here and there a brazier with something cooking on it. Scott kept saying, 'There's a lot of work here yet. We've hardly started.'

Our position with regard to improvements in the front line was curious. 'Old Roy', the GOC[39] 60th Brigade – partly on account of his dislike for Hopkins and partly, I suppose, to teach his battalions to work for themselves – wouldn't allow us to have any say in any work that went on in the front line trenches. We just sent a few men up to help the infantry make their own dugouts etc. Of course it was an impossible system. The infantry at that time had no more idea of revetting a trench or making a dugout that wouldn't collapse than they had of building a steel bridge or of pontooning. A company would start to rebuild a bit of the parapet. The party would do just what the sappers said and if the sapper made a mess of things the old man would come along, see it and immediately slang[40] Hopkins. He really was an impossible man, 'Old Roy'.

As a matter of fact, things usually worked fairly smoothly. Hopkins studiously avoided the brigadier and let us deal amicably with the actual company commanders in the line. We would build them nice mess dugouts and generally run the work of trench improvements for them on the understanding that when the old man came around, the infantry would be doing the work themselves. In a very short time I got to know everybody in the brigade. One could walk all along the trenches in daytime then and visit the various companies and have a meal with them. Often I went around with Schon. He was known everywhere and was generally hailed with 'Hullo, here comes the King of the Islands'. He had a celebrated yarn about the King of the God-damned Islands, which can't be repeated here. He had a great way with the brigadier and could generally smooth things out after a stormy meeting between him and the major.

8th or 9th October 1915

The first event of any real interest happened about a week after I arrived. One morning, two barrels arrived from the CRE with a vague note saying that they contained some stuff for making smoke screens, which we were to experiment with. Major Hopkins sent Schon and Mainsty off with one of the barrels to some secluded area at the back to find out something about the stuff and how one made it work. It was most amusing stuff. The QMS[41] opened the lid of one of the barrels when they first arrived, as he didn't know in the least what they contained. He spilt some of the contents on the ground and to his horror it immediately began to smoke violently, and almost at the same moment, burst into flames, filling the yard with heavy white smoke.

Well, the experts came back having gained some idea of the habits of the stuff, and Scott was called upon to make lots of wooden boxes to hold about 10 pounds each. The scheme was to fire them electrically with just a detonator in the box to break it open.

We had considerable difficulty with the beastly stuff. It would keep catching fire, but at least it was all safely packed away in the boxes and sealed up with clay to keep it quiet.

In the evening the major explained things to us. At least he made us understand what we had to do with the aid of an irregular line drawn on a piece of paper intended to represent the front line, one or two grunts, and some more strokes of the pencil.

We were busy most of the following day getting things ready. Electric detonators had to be tested, long lengths of lead had to be measured out, jointed up so as to form great loops with detonators in series every 70 yards and coiled up on drums ready for carrying. The men had to be chosen, and each party instructed in what they had to do and drilled in doing it.

Each section had to lay a line of smoke boxes along their particular front, just outside the Bosch wire. These boxes were to be let off electrically from the front line the next day to form a smoke screen. It was to form part of the scheme of the feint attack that was coming off. We were going to make a demonstration to try and 'put the wind up the Bosch' and, if possible, make him chary of withdrawing troops to meet our main attack somewhere else. (It was really the last gasp of the Loos offensive.)

That night four heavily laden parties collected at various places along the brigade front line and, after some time had been spent in warning the sentries, they disappeared out over the parapet, through the mess of old jam tins and rubbish that always collects just in front of the parapet of a trench, and out into that mysterious ghostly place that nobody ever saw by daylight except cautiously through a periscope.

It was very queer out there in the dark. Both sides were firing into the darkness as they always do in very quiet parts of the lines. However, no fire came from our own lines just behind us for the sentries had been warned. You could see the flashes of our machine guns further down the line and now and again a Bosch gun would start up and spray bullets just over our heads with that ear-splitting series of cracks that you only hear when a bullet passes close to your head. All the time stray bullets were coming '*crack-crack*' past us from somewhere over there in the darkness.

For miles on either side of this weird, dead strip of land, stretched out a thin band of unexplored mystery, illuminated now and then by piercing white floating lights. These cast cold flickering shadows that grew rapidly brighter, swung round as the light above floated up and was carried by the breeze, shortened to nothing at all when it was overhead and finally lengthened out and disappeared as the darkness came down again like a blanket. The sky was never free of that flickering. There was always a light floating over the line somewhere. Sometimes it would be quite dark and you could just see a faint hovering brightness miles away. Now there would be a 'swish', a trail of sparks going up into the sky and the thing would burst silently, flooding you with a cold, pitiless light:

> What was that over there? Look it's moving its arms about. There's another, a huge fellow. He's coming towards us. Where's my bomb?[42] Does the pin work? Hell, it's only a damned row of willow trees.

But they moved. Everything moved, was swinging around. The dead stunted willow trees turned into parties of Germans who came striding up towards you only to recede again and vanish into the darkness as the light fell to the ground with a fizz behind you and died out.

I had left the drum of cable on the parapet with a sapper whose job it was to see that it unwound properly. The rest of the party advanced through our own wire, each carrying two boxes, a coil of wire connecting them and another coil connecting him with the next man. Once safely over the wire we were going to spread out till all the cable was taut and each man would leave his boxes on the ground so many yards apart and walk in along the cable.

Unfortunately, the beastly cable got caught in the wire and never came out properly. We messed about for some time trying to disentangle it, but it wasn't any good. Eventually I cut the whole lot and we sat down in the long dead grass halfway between our lines and the Bosch to join the whole thing again. It took hours there in the dark. The men were getting fidgety and the lookout men kept seeing Bosch patrols; however, in the end we got it done fairly well.

We got back about five in the morning and went to bed until lunchtime.

When we got up, Hopkins wanted to know all about how we got on. Some hitch or other had happened to each of us but as the show had been postponed for three days it didn't matter.

It was the day after this that my cheerful disregard for machine gun fire and stray bullets was rather modified. I was taking a party of infantry up the railway towards Chaplin Farm for a job of work in the front line. It was about seven o'clock in the evening and there was always rather a lot of firing around that time, especially on the railway. I think they must have paid special attention to the line of that railway with machine guns, hoping to catch ration parties but I never worried. Bullets very seldom seemed to hit anyone. All of a sudden, bullets began to hit the ground just behind us and everyone instinctively dropped to earth.

There was a man hit somewhere behind, and a shout for stretcher bearers. It was one of my own sappers. He was badly hit in the chest, through both lungs apparently. I bandaged him up as well as I could and sent him back down the railway in a truck that fortunately happened to be standing quite close. He died next morning. One of the best men in the section.

After that I was a bit nervous of bullets that came past with a crack, and more still of the rather tired ones that travel slower than sound, so you that can hear them coming. Harvey had been killed. I realised that I also might be killed any time, any moment. It took some time to get accustomed to that idea. I hadn't thought before what a nasty business it was being hit, or of all the mess of blood and dirt, and the smell.

***

12th October 1915

On Tuesday, three days later, we heard that the sham attack really was coming off. It was to be at 10 o'clock the next morning. That evening we laid out some more smoke boxes. This time everything went well except that I had trouble carrying them up. They kept on catching fire round the edges. The stuff must have been mostly phosphorus. We finished early that night and I dropped into one of the company messes for a drink and to while away the time till dawn, for I wanted to test the circuits when it was light to make sure that no wandering Bosch patrol had found them and cut the leads.

It appeared that the day before, great excitement had been caused among the front line garrison by one of our boxes bursting and making a great cloud which blew over our lines. Everyone took it for gas.

13th October 1915

As the hour for the show drew on, our guns put up quite a bombardment. It was the first time I'd heard any sort of bombardment from in front of the guns. Everyone in the front line was in the best of spirits; we were going to make the old Bosch sit up.

In a short time the Bosch started replying and we were surprised at the number of guns he was using. No one thought he had so many opposite us. There was some quite heavy stuff too. Most of it was falling on the support line, but as there was no one there and the trench was in disuse it didn't matter. All the same, there were quite a number of big shells dropping very close to the front line. The whole ground was rocking with their explosions and earth was flying in all directions.

At 10 o'clock, we exploded our smoke boxes from the front line with dynamo exploders, and at the same moment the infantry poked a row of dummies up over the parapet on the ends of bayonets. It was a great joke with them 'the new draft of reinforcements'. Then there was a roar of rifle fire from the Bosch and their artillery bombardment was greatly increased. It was really quite heavy while it lasted, even in the light of subsequent bombardments, only luckily most of it fell on unoccupied trenches. Things began to die down about 2 o'clock and soon afterwards we went home to billets.

***

After that the division settled down for several weeks to the ordinary routine of existence. We carried on with our own little jobs of supervision of trench improvement in the front line: the maintenance of the tramways and the draining and clearing of those communication trenches which had not already collapsed too hopelessly with the rain and mud to be worth repairing.

What a peaceful, happy time we had in those days when one looks back on it. The division was newly out from England and the novelty and thrill of the line were very strong in everyone. It was the same division that had lived together and trained together expectantly for months in the great muddy camps that now lie derelict over Salisbury Plain. All the excitement and the thrill of the last preparations in England, the landing in France and the first sight of the line still hung in men's minds. They felt they were right in the war now and were keen and interested in it.

And there was nothing to dampen their enthusiasm. There was next to no shelling at all – certainly none at night – no mental picture of the vast shell-pitted, deserts of battlefields to warn them that very few would ever live to see the end of the war; not one of us had any knowledge of what real fear was.

The sections used to parade at 8.00 am and be detailed for the day's work. We then went back to the mess for breakfast, while the sappers were marching up to work. About nine we all went up the line on bicycles. Sergeant[43] Perrin generally used to wait behind and ride up with me. We usually went up with Schon for our two sectors of the line were next door to one another. It only took about seven minutes to get up to Joyce's Farm and it was only a mile from there to the front line.

There was always something going on at Joyce's Farm under cover of the orchard. There were trucks being repaired; stores being sorted out and checked etc. The sappers were usually just finishing getting their tools and things out by the time we arrived.

We'd walk on up the track to Chaplin Farm, noting anything that wanted doing to the rails. They were wooden and were always getting worn out. I'd leave Perrin wherever the principal jobs were and go on up the trench to the front line. There was always something going on there. Each platoon worked away at its own little bit of the parapet; 'Old Roy' saw to that. The trouble was to get them to do things properly: to build dugouts that didn't fall in (we used to supply timber already cut to the right lengths and generally one or two sappers to help), to lay sandbags so that the parapets didn't collapse again with the first shower of rain, and to lay trench-boards (supplied by us), so that they didn't either sink in the mud and get lost, or tip up when you trod on the ends. It was difficult and we didn't always succeed. We weren't supposed to give orders but merely to advise.

They were an awfully nice lot, the infantry. There were two battalions who held the sector just in front of Chaplin Farm, the 12th KRRs[44] and the 12th Rifle Brigade. They relieved each other about once a week. There was always a certain amount of rivalry between them as to the amount of work they had done while they were in. Every other week the same platoon would come back to the same bit of line and grumble at the little work the other battalion had done last week.

Often, I would wander along into Schon's sector. The Shropshires and the Oxfordshire and Buckinghamshire Light Infantry were there. I generally find him in some company dugout having a drink and something to eat and spinning yarns. Everybody knew old Schon.

We always got back to lunch at Laventie. We talked mostly about things that happened that morning. Some unfortunate infantry subaltern had laboriously yet artlessly built a tremendous sandbag wall; Schon had pounced on it with a chortle of delight and pulled the whole thing over with one hand.

In the afternoon there was nothing much to do. Scott used to sit in the mess and read magazines, Schon always went to bed. It was always a source of amusement, Schon's going to bed in the afternoon. 'If you will eat a whole bag of walnuts every lunchtime' Scott used to say, 'I suppose you want a bit of a rest afterwards'. I generally went for a ride with Manisty or Jervis.

After tea, Hoppy had a kind of orderly room. He gave orders for tomorrow's work and wanted to know what infantry parties we wanted.

There was always a lot of work going on at night. All jobs that required decent-sized digging parties had to be done after dusk, and a lot of work on the front parapet of course.

We generally went up the line again at about six, chiefly to see the infantry working parties started off on whatever work they were to do for us, and to see that they turned up at the rendezvous at the right time and up to strength in numbers.

It was uphill work getting the infantry to work for us. This was of course very natural: for a long time they had the idea that they'd come out to fight and not to do manual work. It all depended on that the officer you got in charge of the party. There were some platoons who would work like niggers[45] and who gave no trouble whatever. Others gave endless trouble and, in the end, did next to nothing. That was when they had a bad officer who didn't care if the job was done or not, and who let his men see that he didn't care. In general, though, they used to get on pretty well. They all grumbled and called the RE various names, but they did what they were told. In time we learnt all their little dodges for shirking work, and frustrated them pleasantly but firmly. There was the great stuffed sandbag trick. That was when they had to fill sandbags and were given so many each to fill. Some of the men would be finished suspiciously soon and on prodding their nice bulging sandbags, you'd find that they were stuffed full of their remaining bags instead of with earth. In the dark it was very difficult to catch them out. Often if a new officer was with them they would gradually disappear in the darkness.

It was in the evening that the rifle fire sprang up and the strays came over the front parapet and went whining away to the rear where our parties were working, and where the ration parties and columns of men carrying timber and corrugated iron were coming up. It was on and behind Rue Tilleloy that most of the casualties occurred and it was there that most of our work lay.

There was no real urgency about anything at Laventie. If it rained hard, 'Old Roy' wouldn't let us have any infantry to work for us, and there was never any work done on Sundays, nor any night work on Saturday night. We generally went into Estaires on Saturday evenings for dinner at the Hôtel de la Ville. (I don't think Hopkins ever went.) There was usually a merry party there: several officers from other field companies, the 84th and 96th, and some infantry officers.

Estaires was quite a busy little town with several factories and sawmills. We used to buy a good deal of stores there: bolts, timber and ironmongery for our workshops. Very often a fleet of huge canal barges would come up the Lys with road metal for the British or material for the factories and for Armentières further on and gave the place an air of business and activity; it seemed to be thriving in the war.

On Sunday mornings a church parade was generally held in the courtyard of the billet. It consisted of our company, the half battalion of infantry billeted with us and any odd troops that happened to be nearby. We took turns for one of us to attend officially while the others were lazing in the mess, watching the proceedings or were out riding.

Sunday was an excellent day for souvenir hunting. The craze for souvenirs was still very strong. We even went round digging up shell fuses from old shell holes. The trenches opposite Laventie mark to the extreme northern limits of the little advance made during the Battle of Neuve Chapelle in the spring of 1915. My section of the front line was at the end of the original line, dug at the beginning of trench warfare at the start of the war. Further to the right (in Schon, Jervis and Mainsty's sections) the old pre-Neuve Chapelle trenches were still more or less intact some distance behind the actual Front.

The whole system of German and British trenches could be traced, and all the remains of German occupation were there still. Even Hopkins would spend a Sunday afternoon wandering about among the old decaying trenches and long grass, looking for anything German. I can remember him poking away with his great walking stick at the skull of a skeleton that was lying half buried in the trench wall, to see where his teeth had got to.

***

At about the beginning of November the rain really started. In a very short time, the whole of the front line we had taken over from the Indians, that is the whole of the brigade [front] line except mine, had collapsed.

No one had taken the trouble to pass on the lesson learnt in the autumn of 1914, and consequently exactly the same mistake had been made. During the dry weather, beautiful deep trenches had been dug down into the clay with the result that as the water began to rise in the old field drains and ditches, the trenches were all filled. Presently everything below ground level was full of water. All the sandbagging and most of the dugouts which the Indians had built were unfit to stand when the ground was waterlogged and slid quietly in.

There was great alarm and despondency. The CRE – a fussy old 'dugout' – was ordered to do something about it. He had a great notion that all the field ditches were part of an elaborate system of drainage in pre-war days and he set to work to have them all cleared out.

Hopkins borrowed a level[46] from the First Army. He had great difficulty in getting it – apparently, it was the only level in the whole army. We had two expert levellers in the company, and after a good fortnight's work they found there was absolutely no fall anywhere. The ground was flat.

I can't repeat Hoppy's remark about the CRE's ditch cleaning scheme. I've forgotten it. Sardonic old fellow.

Well, we set to work to raise everything above the ground. Communication trenches became avenues, with the trench-boards about ground level, and two high raised parapets on both sides. It meant an enormous amount of digging. The front line became simply a great parapet in places 10 feet high above the ground. All the borrow-pits behind and in front filled up with water, so that the front parapet, the gangway behind and the splinter roof shelters behind that again were cut off by water except where the avenues ran up to meet the front line.

***

14th November 1915

On the 14th November, the division was relieved by the Guards. It was the first time we had seen the Guards and we were very impressed by them. The whole area seemed full of bands and pipers and wonderful looking sergeant majors. We wondered what they thought of us. 'One of those Kitchener Divisions.' In those days a division was summed up by the state of its trenches. What kind of reputation were we going to get in the eyes of these Guards?

Three days later I was sent off with my section to Bac St Maur to take over from the 2nd Field Company of the 8th Division who had been in the line on our left for a very long time and were now going out for a rest.

The billet we took over from the 2nd Field Company was a large cotton mill on the north side of the main street of Bac St Maur, between it and the River Lys just behind. A false floor had been built over the machinery so that the factory was turned into a huge dormitory for the men. All the workshops, sawmills etc. were of course handed over complete by the outgoing company.

The 2nd Field Company had been there a long time and were running a lot of sidelines such as shops for converting old ball bombs into rifle grenades or making concrete slabs for bursting layers[47] of dugout roofs, and several other things. In most of these shops civilian labour was employed, so that I had to take over the supervision of them with my section straight away in order to relieve the other company who were going away at once.

Next morning, Hopkins arrived with the rest of the company. It was arranged that I should carry on with all the odd jobs at Bac St Maur and nearby for the first few weeks and then relieve one of the other sections who were going to live up in an advanced billet – near to their work in the front line.

There were plenty of interesting jobs at Bac St Maur. Apart from the workshops, I had to install an improvised steam heating plant in a sort of advanced hospital, which occupied another cotton mill in the town. I also had to look after certain defence posts between Lys and Fleurbaix.

The steam heating job interested me most of course. I used to go into Armentières several times a week to buy steam piping and fittings. None of us knew anything about steam heating but we got it going in the end. It was a very popular job with the fitters and plumbers in the section. It was one of the few occasions they got to work at their own trades.

The work on the Fleurbaix defences was very boring. It meant going round with the old CRE and messing about repairing the worst pieces of decay in the old trenches that nobody except Kenyon ever seemed to worry about. Most of them had been very badly made and were more or less waterlogged. Besides, the chances of their ever being used seemed so remote that I considered it an awful waste of time.

One of the things left behind by the 2nd Field Company was a large store of explosives of all kinds. I was always very interested in explosives and overhauled the place one day. It was a regular museum. There were a lot of primitive old trench mortars made of pieces of water pipe, things that had been made during the first winter of the war. There was every kind of explosive the army had ever used in the war as well as home-made land mines that some enthusiastic sapper officer had designed months ago and which, like many other things of that kind, had never been used.

This was too good a chance to miss, so I promptly got permission to put the section through a course of explosives and demolitions. There is a fascination about playing with explosives just as there is about playing with fire.

We used every kind of explosive in every kind of way and I learned a lot about demolitions. The NCOs[48] did too and it came in very useful afterwards.

***

The country in front of Bac St Maur was very much the same as at Laventie. Every field was surrounded by deep ditches, lined on both sides by stunted willows which hadn't been pollarded for two years. As a rule the roads were quite open, separated from the fields by these ditches only, except where there were farms and then there would be a bit of hedge along the road and elms all round the farm. There was hardly 200 yards between the farms.

The area was even quieter than the one we had just left. Bac St Maur itself was just 3 miles from the line, yet full of inhabitants. There wasn't a sign of a shell anywhere; the railway was working and lorries using the main road to Armentières travelled with headlights full on. Even the Expeditionary Force canteens ventured into Bac St Maur. I fitted up their shop with shelves and things for them and the mess got a large case of beer in exchange. The farm where Schon and Mainsty lived at Croix Marechal was absolutely intact and civilians were living there. It was only 2,000 yards from the front line.

As regards casualties, however, it was a worse bit of line than the last. The front parapet was not so good and there were lots of places where you had to duck to avoid being spotted in the daytime. It was a bad place for sniping. If you showed your head for a second or two above the parapet, it was two to one that you'd get a bullet through it.

At night the stray bullets were very bad. Being so very quiet, there was a great deal of night firing. It was the only way that the ordinary infantrymen (apart from the recognised sniper) could hope to do any damage to the Bosch. He just fired into the darkness. The Bosch did the same his side.

The war, though, was confined almost entirely to the front line and an area within a thousand yards behind it. Behind that it was peace and there was next to no danger whatever.

***

Time passed very uneventfully for a few weeks. Hopkins, Scott and I were the only people in the mess except in the evenings when Scott generally had one or two others in for a game of poker. Now and then, Mainsty and Schon would come in for the afternoon and we would go into Armentières for tea.

My job gradually took in everything behind the actual front line area, which included the communication trenches. These were looked after by the other sections. There were endless dugouts to be built for the support companies in the posts about a thousand yards behind the front line. There was always work on the posts themselves, keeping them in an occupiable condition.

About the middle of December [1915] there was a craze for trying to pick up Bosch working parties in no man's land by means of searchlights. A field company carries two acetylene searchlights as part of its equipment. We had never used the things before. The mirror reflectors within the searchlights were all rotten – all the silvering had come off them. However, the brigadier had ordered it.

I took the whole outfit up as far as I could get in a limber just after dark and from there we carried the things up the road to Boutillerie by hand. They were pretty bulky and took about eight men each to take up all the various parts, lamps, cylinders etc.

It was the only time I ever remember the Bosch to do any shelling at night while we were in that part of the world. We had to take refuge several times behind houses along the road. There were only one or two shells really, but we weren't used to shells at night at all.

Everyone was very interested in the experiment when we got to the front line. We were going to have one in each of the two battalion fronts in the brigade. The idea was to pick up a [German] wiring party outside the front line opposite and turn all our available machine guns onto them. Of course, we all expected that the Bosch would fire back at the lights like blazes.

Everything was ready and we turned the lights on and searched about. We didn't pick up anything except a row of willow trees, which wasn't to be wondered at, as the range was only about a hundred yards and the Bosch front line was about 200 [yards]. However, it was quite fun and any little novelty of that kind was very welcome.

We were disappointed in the disdainful silence in which the Bosch received us. There wasn't a shot fired. After about a quarter of an hour, though, a huge electric searchlight opened up from behind the Bosch line and swept the whole country. What a feeling of superiority the old Bosch must have had, sitting there in front of that impregnable Aubers Ridge and watching our rotten little efforts.

***

21st December 1915

On the 21st December, I went on leave. I think Hoppy arranged it specially so that I could get the Christmas leave as I was the baby of the mess.

I went from La Gorgue, I remember, at half past one in the morning, having been driven from Bac St Maur in the front of a limber.

While I was away, the 60th Brigade was relieved by the 59th and after a week's rest, went in again a little further to the right.

The division was then holding the line with only two brigades and a third resting behind. Each brigade had two battalions in the line and two in the farms and posts about 1,000 to 2,000 yards behind. I got back just after our brigade, the 60th, had taken over. It was 30th December.

Next morning, Schon and I moved up with our sections to an estaminet at Croix Blanche. It was a quaint little place. Two little barns for the sections and a little [officers'] mess in the estaminet. You went through the front public room where the beer was sold and loud voices raised, then through the bedroom where the people of the house slept (all of them, mother, father, daughter and fiancé or somebody and a grandfather or two) and finally into our room which served as a mess and a sleeping room for Schon, myself and two officers of the brigade trench mortar battery.

We had a most amusing time there. The two trench mortar people were a priceless couple. The OC was a subaltern of about 19 [years old] who swelled with self-importance. The administration of his battery caused us endless fun. Whenever he got a straff[49] from the staff captain for not sending some return, he'd get quite excited and call for his clerk who knew less than he did about the interior economy of the battery. Then a large box would be brought in and they would tip the whole of the contents – stationery, forms, and envelopes and things – out on the floor. The missing form could never be found. I'm afraid we used to rag the fellow mercilessly. His clothes were always getting lost just when a message came to say that the staff captain wanted to see him at once. Old fat Schon used to sit by the fire and chuckle.

Our work was now entirely in the front line. Schon had the left battalion and I had the right. Jervis lived in a farm down the road at Croix Lescornex, but he used to mess with us. He was working on the communication avenues.

It only took a quarter of an hour to walk up to the front line from our billet, where civilians were still living.

We did practically nothing but heighten and improve the front parapet. The day's work consisted of filling in the timber revetment frames that we had wired the previous night, securing new frames into position ready for wiring, and filling sandbags for use on the top of the parapet. Directly it got dark enough, we would get outside in front of the parapet.

At night the other half of the section would come up just after dark, get outside and drive in pickets on the forward slope of the parapet. The revetting frames – generally about 6 feet high by 3 [feet] wide – supported the inside wall of the parapet and these were anchored to the pickets with stout wire. The last foot or so of the parapet was finished off with sandbags so that if a field gun shell hit the parapet the frames and wire wouldn't be cut.

There were also large carrying parties every night to get all the revetting frames, trench-boards and pickets up.

Night work was the worst. Bullets used to rain across Rue Pétillon, which seemed to catch all the strays coming over the front line. There were lots of casualties among men walking along Rue Pétillon. Further up, nearer the line, you came under the shelter of the front parapet and were more or less safe.

The front line was the same kind of place here as at Laventie. Each company had its mess and you could walk along and see all your friends in the infantry. It was a sociable place. A Company of the 12th KRR were the people I knew best then. Charworth-Musters was with them for a long time. I forget which platoon he had. It was miles the best for working parties anyway. They were always cheerful and willing to do a bit of digging.

My battalion sector, stretching from Bond Street on the right to a few hundred yards to the left of where Rue Delvas crossed the front line, was particularly interesting in having a river through the front line under a bridge, which supported the main parapet. Everyone from the chief engineer of the 3rd Corps downwards took a special interest in the River Laies. Its height had to be measured and reported on. When the Laies rose, everything was under water: roads, trenches, fields. We had all sorts of pumping schemes. Several communications trenches had little pumping plants of their own to try and keep the trench-boards at the bottom above water level.

***

One Sunday morning, Schon and I, having nothing much to do, went for a walk along the front line to the right, all along our old bit of line in front of Laventie which the Guards were then holding. It was a lovely morning and there might hardly have been a war on. There were only one or two rifle shots the whole morning and we never heard a shell at all.

We walked about 4 miles along the front line without even having to duck our heads once. It was just one long trench board track behind a great high parapet.

We all had the idea in those days that you could walk right along the front line from the sea to Switzerland and it was all just like this. The thought pleased us a lot and we calculated how long it would take.

***

On the night of the 5th January, Jervis was found dead by the side of Rue Pétillon – shot through the head by a stray bullet. He had been up to see a party of his men working in Cordonnerie Avenue and was coming back by himself without an orderly. We buried him next day at a little battalion cemetery quite close.

Poor little Jervis. I always remember how he used to sing to himself while he was going to bed in our room at Laventie. It was nearly always the same thing: a verse out of some popular song about when this bloody war is over…

> When this bloody war is over,
> Oh, how happy I shall be.
> When I get my civvy clothes on,
> No more soldiering for me.

He was always making plans, too, about what he was going to do after the war.

***

It was a few days after Jervis' death that we first got rumours of being relieved and of going back into rest. I for one didn't want to a bit. I pictured long route marches and drilling, 'playing at soldiers' Schon called it. I had never been with an infantry unit on the march, in fact, I had never been with one at all except when it was in line.

I was quite nervous of this 'playing at soldiers'. There would be 'march discipline' as per Field Service Regulations and all that sort of thing instead of the free life we had been living.

***

10th January 1916

On the 10th January, we moved back to Company HQ at Bac St Maur and found a new officer there to fill Jervis' place. He was a quiet sort of fellow called Miers and had been a long time in Brazil.

Next morning, we all paraded in the road outside the billet at seven thirty. There was a lot of chasing about to get all the section transport in its right place. Each section kept its transport in separate spots.

At last we got into line ready to move off. My section being No. 1 marched in front, the other sections behind and the headquarters transport, pontoons, trestle wagons, watercart etc. in the rear. Each section had thirty-seven dismounted men, two mounted NCOs and three drivers for the two wagons. Eight of the sappers rode on bicycles.

I had no idea what a big thing a field company looks on the road. It takes up a quarter of a mile of road space. First of all come the little squad of dismounted men of No. 1 Section, then eight men on bicycles, then the tool cart with its four horses and the forage cart, then the next section and so on. After that come the two great pontoon wagons, each with six horses or mules and the trestle wagon, and then a couple of GS[50] wagons with rations and forage etc. Lastly an odd assortment of vehicles which the company had collected unlawfully from time to time: a pony trap for mess gear, a couple of old French carts extracted from some ruined farm etc.

It wasn't half as bad as I thought, in fact, it was rather fun on the whole. Every hour we'd stop for ten minutes to see that the transport and the horses were alright, and to have a bit of a blow.[51]

Old Hopkins rode a little way ahead, all by himself with his curved pipe sticking fiercely out of his mouth. His groom rode just behind. Sometimes when he got tired of riding, he would give his horse to his groom, get out his old stick which he always had with him, and stride on ahead.

The front rank of my section used to talk about him among themselves: 'I wonder what the old major thinks about all the time.'

We got to the billets we were to occupy for the night at about 12.30 pm. One of us, Mainsty I think, had been sent in ahead to find the farms we had been allotted and arrange for the sections and horses to be fitted in. We were split up into two farms half a mile apart on two roads that crossed the railway just left of Strazeele station.

In an hour's time everything was fixed up and the company settled in. Each section was run more or less as a separate unit; Hopkins was always very keen on that. A section of a field company should be able to move off as a separate detachment at a moment's notice. They each ran their own cookhouse and kept their own reserve of rations. We went round the sections and saw that they had decent billets, that they had a place to cook, and that the horses were alright.

That afternoon there was nothing much to do. We went along into Vieux Berquin and bought some things for the mess.

There was a lot of talk about what was going to happen to us. We knew that we were going on to Steenbecque tomorrow but after that nobody knew anything. The only thing we had to go on was a remark that old General Schreiber made when he inspected the divisional RE a week or two before. He was a bad man. Nobody liked him. He was the chief engineer of the corps. The gist of his speech had been:

> I don't know anything about you. I've never seen you before. You may think you know all about the war, but you don't. I'm told you are going to a place where you will find out what the war is really like.

We were very indignant about him. Still even if he had meant that we were going to the Salient, we certainly weren't going in that direction yet.

For a long time, I had wanted to go to the [Ypres] Salient. It was such a famous place and one certainly ought to see it, just for a short time of course. One had heard so many stories about Ypres and the Salient. About a week before, I had had a letter from Grindley. He was up there somewhere. He talked about Hellfire Corner and the Menin Road. I wanted to be up there, just to have been there and to have seen all the famous places that people seemed to talk about with awe.

***

12th January 1916

In the morning, we pushed on to Steenbecque. The billets were on the by-road running from the village to the station. We stayed there for ten days. The weather was pretty good and I thoroughly enjoyed it. First of all, it was on a bit of a hill, and we hadn't seen any sort of a hill or even a rise in the ground, except the Aubers Ridge for four months. The air seemed better, even on that little bit of a rise.

We used to do a bit of drill and physical training in the mornings and have the whole of the afternoons to ourselves. Generally, we went into Hazebrouck. You could buy a lot of things there. There was an old Belgian who kept a sweet shop just off the square, and who ran a little select pub for officers in a room behind. I don't know why he wasn't caught by the APM[52].

There were always several people we knew there. The 60th Brigade were billeted behind Morbeque and they all flocked into Hazebrouck in the afternoon for dinner.

The rumour of our going to the Salient was getting stronger every day. Apparently, we were going to form part of a new corps which was being formed.

On the 19th, I woke up feeling very seedy. We'd been having an oyster feast in Hazebrouck the night before, and I thought I'd got poisoned. Mainsty was bad too, with a rash all over him. We both stayed in bed all day.

Leckey the doctor came to see us on the 21st. He said it was only flu and we'd be able to get up the next day – in fact we'd have to, as the division was moving again, to north of Ypres. Well, we were actually going to the Salient then. No one else wanted to go much. Everyone seemed to have evil forebodings.

***

22nd January 1916

From the 22nd till the end of the month, we lived in a farm about a mile north of Sylvestre Cappel on the east of the road.

There was very little to do. We practised demolitions with our sections and did squad drill in the mornings. In the afternoon I went for rides or walks, generally with Mainsty.

One afternoon we went to Cassel, Mainsty and I, and climbed up to the casino[53] terrace to see the view. The village of Cassel lies almost at the top of the extraordinary hill that rises straight up out of the flat country like a great ant heap. Just above the village stands the casino, then Second Army Headquarters.

As you come out on to the terrace after climbing a long flight of steps the view suddenly appears over the top and seems to strike you in the face. The country unrolls in every direction like a great map. I've never seen anything like it. The cold wind always whistling round the corners of the casino gives one the feeling of being perched up at some great altitude.

It was pretty clear that afternoon, and we could see for a great distance before the haze eventually obscured things. To the north-west lay the white line of the dunes, to the north the long straight road radiating away and ending in the spire of Wormhoudt. Further east the sky was overcast and a great black cloud hung there, making the land underneath look dark and cold in comparison with the brightness elsewhere.

I had a map and we started trying to spot places in the direction we knew we were bound for sooner or later. There was the spire of Steenvoorde about four miles away and beyond that we could see the long road stretching away towards Poperinghe. Yes, we could see the three spires of Poperinghe. Somewhere beyond there, hidden in the shadow of that great black cloud lay Ypres: the famous place, about which there were so many stories of shells and death, where all the heavy and critical fighting on the British front had taken place. A place of mystery, impossible to visualise.

And further to the north ... A fortnight before, in a drawer in the room at Strazeele we had used as a mess, I had found an old copy of [Sir John] French's despatch, giving an account of the Second Battle of Ypres. I had been thrilled by it. I had tried to picture the terror of the first gas attack and the bombardment of Ypres, but it was the account of the fighting to the north around Pilckem and Boesinghe that had fascinated me most. I have never met anyone who could give any details of it. Only vague scraps. There was practically no one left to tell the tale.

Reading the official account produced a fantastic and horrible mental picture of the relieving battalions marching up across the Yser Canal with no protection whatever in an atmosphere still hazy with chlorine, marching past roadsides lined with gaping men slowly dying of suffocation, up to meet a thin green mist that was rolling anew down the slopes from the ridge and not understanding it – not knowing what had happened.

We were going up there, right on the left flank of the British Army. We were going to that mysterious place that lay in front of Elverdinghe whence those lights used to rise and shine through the trees at night that we used to watch from the damp oak woods last autumn.

As we peered into the distance from the top of Cassel, I realised for the first time what a strange glamour there was about Ypres and the Salient and all their associations, something that made the whole place different from the rest of the Front.

***

It was just about then that we had heard about joining the new 14th Corps which was to be composed of the Guards Division, ourselves and the 6th. The story got about that Lord Cavan – who had commanded the Guards Division since the Battle of Loos and had taken over from our division at Laventie – had written a letter to the [British] Army reporting on the excellent state of the trenches. This was astonishing to us as we were rather despondent about them ourselves. It had apparently made our name as a division.

A few months later, he was given the command of the new 14th Corps which was to be a sort of crack corps and was going to hold the left flank of the [British] Army during the spring campaign. He had been allowed to pick what divisions he liked from among those that were available. And he had chosen us as one of his divisions.

This was fine, and the division began to take a pride in itself. Still, we were going to about the most dangerous spot in the British front; a place where the Bosch had tried to break through before and seemed to be thinking of doing it again.

Chapter 2

THE CANAL (FEBRUARY–APRIL 1916)

1st February 1916

On the 1st February, I was sent up with about twenty other officers from the brigade to live with the 14th Division, which we were eventually going to relieve, so as to learn something of the way of things in the Salient before the whole Division came up. I was sent to the 61st Field Company and the others went to various battalions of the brigade of the 14th Division.

We went up by bus from Steenvoorde along the long *pavé*[54] road to Poperinghe. The country became more and more familiar: the oak woods, the hop fields and the dirty little herbergs[55] or estaminets with their odd unpronounceable names.

Then Poperinghe again, just the same as ever with Ginger's tea shop and the theatrical posters of the 6th Division Fancies. But then we went on past the station and out of the area I knew. Now we were actually going up the famous 'Wipers Road'.

***

The 61st Field Company lived at Branhoek. It was really right out of their area, which lay further north, but the 14th Division had only recently side-stepped their front to the left to take over from the old 49th Division, which had been holding the canal sector when I was with the entrenching battalion, and the various units hadn't yet moved their billets over.

They wanted to know all about the 20th Division and were delighted to have a listener to whom they could pour out their own tale of woe. The 14th Division were a sister division to ours and all their battalions belonged to the same regiments as ours. From the very start they had been unlucky. Instead of being sent to a quiet bit of line at first, as we had been, they had been sent straight to Ypres directly they came out from England in June 1915. There they had come in for all the summer fighting and had lost very heavily, chiefly through an incompetent staff. A whole brigade, for instance, had actually been marched up the Menin Road in fours in broad daylight, under the very eyes of the Bosch.

The first time they were put in to hold the line by themselves at Hooge, they had been met by the very first Bosch liquid fire attack and had lost their trenches. The 6th Division had to come and retake them.

After that they had lost other trenches and had been pushed to one side while the 6th Division again had to come and retake these. And so it had gone on. They were always in the line, they knew they were a bad division and the knowledge didn't make them any better.

On the top of it all, the 6th Divisional commander had then been given command of the 6th Corps, which they were both under. He despised the poor 14th [Division] and was always holding the 6th [Corps] up as a model in front of them.

For months they had longed to get away from the Salient. At the beginning of December, they had had definite orders to move to Mediterranean and there was great rejoicing. A few days later, however, their hopes were dashed to the ground and they were sent back to Railway Wood and Hooge, places that they shuddered to think of, only to come in for the great gas attack of 19th December 1915.

They were an unlucky division altogether and their moral was pretty low. They never had a chance.

The 61st Field Company reflected the general despondency. They were continually bringing tales and reminiscences of Hooge and Railway Wood and the fighting of the last autumn; of their horses and transport being smashed up at night on the roads during the periodic 'Road Straffs' that the Bosch went in for; of back billets being shelled; of the famous 17-inch howitzer dropping shells into Ypres and Vlamertinghe and holding up all the traffic for hours on end. They had a lot of stories about that howitzer, stories that were handed on from division to division for years afterwards. They told of the shell that went right through the Ramparts and burst the other side; also of the single shell that killed 120 men at Elverdinghe and so on. They always came back to the same theme, a longing to get away from the Salient. They had had so many false rumours that even now they didn't quite believe that we really were going to relieve them.

***

That evening I went up with Fenwick, one of their subalterns to the canal[56] bank, where they had one section living in dugouts. There I was to stop the night and go round all their jobs while it was dark.

It was getting dark when we started off, riding on the front part of a limber. The nightly stream of transport was just beginning to move up the great Main Road under cover of dusk.

The moon had just risen as we drifted through Vlamertinghe wedged in an apparently endless column of traffic creeping up towards the line and the ruined steeple of the church stood out in an odd silhouette. It was very clear and still and for a long time there was no sound but the monotonous subdued rumble of a thousand wheels and horse hoofs on the muddy *pavé* and the jingling of harnesses.

All at once came a salvo from a battery quite close to the road. It broke the stillness like the crack of a whip, and the echoes went rolling away to the eastward. Then stillness again.

We turned off up the Brielen road out of the main stream of traffic, turned to the right at Brielen where most of the roofs were off and half the walls down, then to the left up a road with filled-in shell holes to Essex Farm where we met the Ypres–Boesinghe road with its broad *pavé* and double lines of beeches.

Beyond this loomed the long black ridge of the raised canal bank, likewise lined with rows of beeches, stretching away into the darkness right and left.

We turned to the left along the Boesinghe road and soon pulled up opposite a gap in the wall of the canal bank, which I afterwards knew as the approach to Bridge 6. Here there was a great tramping of feet and wagons were being unloaded. No traffic went further north along the road. There were shell holes in it and I could see a tree lying across.

We crossed the little plank bridge over the Yperlee stream that runs just behind the canal bank. Immediately on the other side of the stream a long trench-boarded gangway had been cut in the side of the canal bank which rose about 15 feet high above it. A few yards along we came to Buckel's dugout running into the bank: a tunnel of semi-circular section about 6 feet high in the middle and built of heavy sections of corrugated steel – the usual 'Elephant' dugout. The entrance to it opened straight on to the gangway.

There was the usual talk about what stores Buckel wanted sent up from Brandhoek, the usual grouse about the infantry working parties not turning up, and other topics of conversation that always crop up whenever an officer from the rear billets of a field company turns up at the dugouts of its forward section. Outside on the gangway an endless tramping of feet went on: men shuffling along in the dark and carrying parties passing one another on the narrow trench-boards.

After supper we went out to see the work they had in hand in the trenches out beyond the canal. We walked along the gangway to the cutting through the bank, turned through it and came out on to a sagging wooden bridge with the still water of the 100-foot-wide canal some 10 feet below us.

As we emerged from the cutting in the bank into the hollow trough of the canal it was as if a door had been closed and all the multitude of night noises shut out. The rattle of wagons and harnesses on the Boesinghe road and the voices of men died away to a whisper. All was still; not a puff of wind penetrated the double walls of trees on either bank. Only the soft padding of men walking silently to and fro across the wooden bridge.

The moon was shining straight down on the glassy water of the canal and, about a mile or so down, stood the jagged, silhouetted outlines of the spires and walls of Ypres itself. The single remaining side of the great tower of the cathedral with its one pinnacle and the long, broken window near the top seemed to be stretching upward like a huge arm out of the ruins of the town.

Bridge after bridge in various stages of decay lay strewn across the water on both sides of us. Some were mere rows of stumps sticking out of the water, casting skeletal shadows on its surface. On either bank the white stalks of two rows of dead and dying trees – all leaning permanently over to the east from the pressure of the west wind – stretched away into the dim cold moonlight as far as we could see.

Down towards Ypres, little yellow lights twinkled out from the east bank and shone on the water. The whole place along there was honeycombed with dugouts. There must be thousands living in those burrows in the banks, and yet everything was curiously still.

Why did it seem so strange up here on the canal? Why was it so different from the nights at Laventie or Fleurbaix? The whole atmosphere seemed different. Occasionally a field gun fired from somewhere behind. Even that sounded different from the guns that used to fire at Laventie. There was that protracted rattling after noise of the shell passing over the long rows of trees along the canal. It was the first time I had heard guns firing at night. They didn't do it at Laventie.

Where was all the endless haphazard rifle fire that showed that everything was normal and as it should be, both sides standing in the trenches and firing into the dark to keep their hands warm? It was missing. Things weren't nice and settled and permanent like they were in the quiet front we'd come from. There seemed to be an air of expectancy. Everyone unconsciously waiting for some unknown thing to happen out there in the moonlight.

Only to the north were there any signs of war. A machine gun, sometimes two or three together, were firing intermittently and traversing round. Little short bursts that broke up the stillness for a few seconds and then stopped. 'There's Mad Alec on the go again, damn him', said Buckel. 'He's traversing across [Bridge] 6D. He caught a whole party last night. I was there. They dropped off the bridge into the water.'

We walked on up to the rickety tramway to Lancashire Farm. Several times we had to lie on our faces while machine gun bullets whizzed by.

The country was different from the other side of the canal. It was all open and covered with short rough grass. You could see quite a long way in the moonlight, and there didn't seem to be any tree or hedge whatever. Just an open moorland. Here and there were lines of barbed wire or old trenches.

They were working on a line of little posts or 'grouse butts' as they called them, just in front of Lancashire Farm.

There was quite a slope up from the canal to this point. The Bosch held the Pilckem Ridge and dominated the whole country. He could see everything that went on in the daytime both east and west of the canal. If he saw any new work, any trenches dug, he would shell them to pieces, and the 14th Division had apparently given up the attempt to build faster than he could destroy.

I didn't sleep well that night after we got back to the canal at about midnight. I hadn't often slept in a dugout before. There was a gun that fired at regular intervals and kept me awake, and there was that continuous tramp of feet and muttered words from the trench-boards outside. I kept listening to the rattle of the machine guns to the north.

Next morning, we went round and I was shown the dugouts and accommodation that was available for us when we arrived. There was just one long line of dugouts in the west bank. They looked out westward on the Yperlee Stream and the little ragged bit of hedge on the far side of the heart. Beyond that was the Boesinghe road with its lines of thin, leaning trees. Half of them broken and many were smashed down altogether. The Bosch did quite a lot of shelling that morning. They came whizzing over the top of the bank and burst just beyond the road. Further down towards Ypres there were great black things that burst in the air over the canal with a tremendous metallic crash.

In the afternoon I went back to Brandhoek and Major Mackenzie the OC took me round to see the new camp they were building for themselves near Steentje Mill behind Elverdinghe. Brandhoek was too far away and out of the area. We would probably go straight to the new camp when we actually took over.

What a strange coincidence it was, my coming back to the very area I had been in before with the Entrenching Battalion.

***

3rd February 1916

Next day, I went back to join the company at St Sylvestre Cappel. While I had been away, Mainsty – who had never got on very well with old Hopkins – had been sent to the 84th Field Company in exchange for Watson, one of the fellows in my batch at the Shop.

I missed Mainsty badly. We used to hit it off very well together. We were said to be very much alike. I was always mistaken for him.

A few days later, we moved to Watou and on the 11th February marched through Poperinghe and up the Elverdinghe Road to our new camp at A18 d 9.6 (Sheet 28). No. 3 and 4 Sections with Miers and Watson went up by train from Poperinghe in the evening and marched up the canal road from Ypres to the dugouts at Bridge 6.

The camp at Dromore Corner consisted of a farm in which we started our mess and a lot of huts for the sections. The workshops and horse lines were in the little wood east of the road just before you go down past Veulle Seule Cabaret.

There was a broad-gauge railway running in a loop right round the camp, which looked rather ominous, as if we might one morning find an enormous gun sitting there in the act of loosing off.

Schon was on leave at the time so that there were only Hopkins, Scott and myself at the camp. Watson and Miers were up on the canal bank. Everyone was very sleepy; we'd been marching most of the day from Watou in a storm of hail and sleet and were all soaked through.

***

12th February 1916

That night when the infantry of the 60th Brigade were marching up to relieve the battalions of the 14th Division in the trenches – from Fusilier Farm to the end of the British front at F35 on the canal – the Bosch attacked and drove the unfortunate garrisons of the wretched, isolated bits of trench out of their line and back on the columns of the 60th Brigade who were coming up.

It was a pitch dark night and the confusion was terrible. Somehow or other the newcomers managed to drive the enemy out everywhere, except the last trench of all (F35), which ran out all by itself along the canal bank. How they found the various bits of front line I don't know. There were no communication trenches up to them and the ground was so caught up by shell holes that it was hard to tell a trench when you found it.

The two sections of ours on the canal bank had arrived about an hour before. Watson got orders to man all the bridges and prepare them for demolition. He had a fairly hectic night. Miers was rather a broken reed, and there was more or less a barrage on the canal bank which did not tend to make his job any the more pleasant in the inky darkness.

All that night, we were sleeping peacefully back at the camp and it wasn't until the following afternoon when I cycled up to see Watson that I heard anything of what had happened. That was about three in the afternoon. I left again in half an hour and had got as far as Murat Farm when heavy shelling started again up towards Boesinghe and soon worked down the canal completely, screening it from view. The Bosch were attacking again.

One of the jobs that my section had been made responsible for was the maintenance of the tramways from the rear, up as far as the canal. As soon as I got back and had had something to eat, Scott and I set out with the two sections to see what we could do in the way of keeping the tramway in order from Mordacq crossroads to the canal at Bridge 6W.

We went up the road past Hospital Farm and Fantasia Farm to Dawson's Corner and so on, up to our company store dump at Belmont Farm. Sure enough, Dawson's Corner lived up to the reputation that the 14th Division had handed on to us of it. Salvos of four shells were bursting there every minute or so. However, we got through alright, and having collected trucks and rails at the dump, we went on up the tramway towards the canal.

That night was the first time I was really frightened. It was our first experience of night shelling, and of that awful sinking feeling of abject terror when one hears a shell coming and waits for the blinding flash and the metallic rending noise of the burst. In the darkness one seems to lose that wonderful ability to judge from the sound of a shell as it comes through the air where it is going to burst.

It was a futile job trying to keep the tramway functioning through that night. Whole lengths were cut out behind us as soon as we finished one break and went on to the next. At last when things were a bit quieter we left Sergeant Perrin in charge and went up to see Watson on the canal bank. The Bosch had attacked again, twice that afternoon up on the left, but the brigade was apparently still holding out. Watson had just come back from a visit to his bridges. He had also been along to see Brigade Headquarters along the canal bank near Bridge 5. On the whole, they seemed pleased with the way things had gone, but people were very dissatisfied with the way the 14th Division artillery had not backed us up. Our own artillery hadn't arrived.

We got to bed at about 2.00 am and had been asleep about half an hour when we were woken up with a 'swish', followed by a resounding crash. They were shelling our camp. About twelve shells came over at intervals of a minute, then silence and we turned over and dozed off again. Every three quarters of an hour, the same thing happened. It was a most miserable night: very cold, freezing hard. One was woken up by a burst and waited tensely for the next one, wondering where the last had fallen, how near. A minute later the next would arrive: 'That was quite close, surely.' By this time, you were sitting up in bed, shivering with cold in the little draughty hut. Was it near enough to warrant getting up to see if everything was alright? We'll wait for the next one anyway. You felt so high up in your bed, so exposed. What a rotten, thin thing a hut was.

Hopkins was very annoyed with the brigade staff – with 'Old Roy' in particular. For a whole week afterwards, no sound scheme of defence was decided upon. We did what we were told to do – which consisted chiefly of making the brigadier comfortable. We did a few odd bits of work on communication trenches here and there, but there was no settled programme for dealing with the terrible state of the line.

Every trench was in ruins. The front line – instead of being a nice high continuous parapet behind which you could walk for miles in daylight without being seen (which was our only idea of a front line) – consisted of a few miserable bits of crumbling trench, with no trench-boards at the bottom and no revetting to hold up the sides. There were just isolated posts, the remains of an attempt long ago to form a continuous trench line, nearly all of which had been allowed to collapse. There were no communication trenches leading up to them, and many men – small ration parties etc. – lost their way trying to find the various little posts and walked straight through the gaps into the Bosch lines, never to be heard of again. Once a platoon was led up at night by a guide to its particular post (F29 or E28 or whichever it was), there they had to stay until they were relieved. There was no stirring in the daytime. Nothing could be done to make themselves comfortable, no digging. The Bosch was sitting on the Pilckem Ridge watching for any movement, any signs of fresh earth thrown up, to turn his guns onto it and destroy it.

***

Things were quiet. The Bosch didn't attack again. The division had done well. A letter of congratulation came down from the 14th Corps from Lord Cavan himself. Still there was an air of foreboding and tense expectancy. The nights were so unnaturally quiet. Both sides seemed waiting. It was in this same sector, ten months before, that the greatest of all horrors of the war had taken place.

19th February 1916

On the morning of 19th February, Schon came back from leave. I went up to the canal bank that afternoon meaning to have a look at some repairs that were going on at Bridge 6W and at dusk to show Schon around the line.

I left him at Watson's dugout at Bridge 6 and went along the gangway to [Bridge] 6W. When I had got about halfway the Bosch barrage started – on the line of the canal bank. It was no good trying to go on. A rain of shells was skimming the top of the bank, some striking the trees and blowing them down, some falling into the canal and raising mountains of water, others dropping in the fields just behind. The little tramline running just behind the Yperlee was being completely torn up. At the same time the 'enfilade battery' was sweeping the canal bank gangway with shrapnel so that there was no cover at all except in the crazy dugouts in the bank. I crawled into one of those and waited for two hours until it stopped.

There were 400 men killed that afternoon in dugouts along the bank. The next three dugouts I found on my right were completely blown in and five on the left. The five men of ours who had been working on Bridge 6W were all killed.

By the time I got back to Bridge 6 and safety it was getting dark. Hoppy, Scott and Schon were there in Watson's dugout with trench maps and orders from the brigade. The Bosch had attacked the whole of the front line from F34 to F30. The only trenches left on the east side of the canal were S32 and a little bit of trench called Wyatt's Lane. Behind that was the canal, a 100-feet wide with no bridge across it north of [Bridge] 6D.

Schon and I set out almost at once with instructions to meet a party of infantry at [Bridge] 6W and take them up to Wyatt's Lane to start work on linking up by a trench from there to S32.

It was a dark night, and that journey seemed endless. The trench-boards along the gangway were old and worn out. They were full of holes and steps and there were trees lying across that had been felled by the recent bombardment. One had to feel one's way around the traverses and corners, barging into silent figures in the dark or stepping almost into the Yperlee to allow other parties of men to pass. The 'enfilade gun' of which the outgoing division had spoken was busy that night. It fired from somewhere to the north and raked the gangway with shrapnel.

All the way there was that long endless double row of white skeleton trees along the top of the bank above. As we went north, the trees became more and more knocked about. They were lying all over the place. The dugouts in the bank became fewer and flimsier, and the ground from being more or less grass covered was now a stale black earth.

We picked up the party of men at Bridge 6W and went on as far as [Bridge] 6D. This we had to cross and there was Mad Alec to be contended with. He was very active. We had heard him all the way as we came along. In the cutting in the bank leading to the bridge we halted and waited for the next burst of fire. There he was: '*crack crack crack*' traversing the bridge just in front. There was nothing for it. It was no good waiting, or the men behind would get cold and 'windy'. Directly the machine gun ceased we made a bolt for it, trusting to luck that we could get the whole party over before the next burst of fire. It was a rickety wooden bridge about 10 feet above the water. Down below there was a scum of wreckage of all kinds that had drifted down and collected against the trestles. It was bad to look down there.

All at once that sinking feeling. '*Crack crack*' like pistol shots close to the ear, making your head sing. He was at it again. We ran the remaining distance to the east bank headlong. He was firing high.

On the east bank we continued for another 1,200 yards along Fargate Trench, the only connecting link to the men still holding the little post at Wyatt's Lane. If the west bank of the canal was knocked about, the east bank was far worse. It seemed in the darkness to be a mess of tumbled earth. Hardly a tree was standing. They seemed to be in splintered pieces everywhere.

Along the top of the bank ran what remained of Fargate. It was nowhere more than 3 feet deep and had had a direct hit every few yards. Here and there the trench-boards still existed and afforded a more or less firm footing, but there were sudden gaps where you could sink up to your thighs in deep mud. There were no dugouts anywhere along here. There can have been no cover from view whatever. The forward slope of the bank was under direct observation from in front and the inner slope could be seen and swept with machine guns from the Bosch trenches at the bend in the canal up by F35.

We took about three quarters of an hour to get up to Fargate. Mad Alec was on the go pretty well continuously, playing straight down the trench or sweeping the canal below. At the same time the trench was blocked with men. There was nothing in front except the Bosch so that it was manned as a front line. The Durhams (the divisional pioneer battalion) were there too. They were working on the trench trying to clear it. Here and there in empty stretches of the trench, the rats scuttled from under one's feet and fought and squeaked on the uneven mounds of earth which formed the sides.

At last we arrived at the spot where Wyatt's Lane jutted out from Fargate. Musters was there and his Company Commander, Captain Radford. Everybody was very quiet for the Bosch could only be 20 or 30 yards away. Hopkins and Scott turned up a few minutes later and we deliberated in whispers. Musters said he had come across an old trench a few nights before that seemed to run backwards parallel to Fargate from the end of Wyatt's Lane towards S32. If we could get that fit for men to occupy, it would do as an outpost to protect Fargate behind. Then he disappeared and we forgot about him as we crept out to examine Wyatt's Lane and look for the beginning of the old trench. We found it, but it didn't look at all hopeful. It was only just traceable as a hollow running through the surrounding black mass of mud and water-filled shell holes. We sank into the bottom of it in some places up to our waists and the mud stank.

Suddenly there was a faint clicking of rifles and whispering, 'Who was that out there?' [and] 'Yes, I saw something move. Look, there he is again.' [and] 'I wish we knew whereabouts the new Bosch trenches were.'. Yes there was somebody out there. He was coming towards us from the direction of S32. Every rifle was pointed at him and no one dared to hail him lest the Bosch should hear. It was Musters. How he hadn't been shot a dozen times by the garrison of Fargate trench behind, staring out into the night with nothing behind them but the black water of the canal and the Bosch prowling anywhere in front of them, I don't know. He had been right along the old trench. Yes, it did run into S32.

We got the infantry working party out along the trench. They had to wade through feet of mud and I suppose the splashing must have been heard by the Bosch. The ground was skimmed by machine-gun bullets from three or four guns together almost incessantly. For nearly an hour we had to crouch down in the mud-filled hollows that had once been a trench. All about were the remains of former occupants; one could feel them with one's feet down in the mud below; arms and legs stuck out of the loose mud by one's side in the last stages of decay and as the rain of bullets went on, we crouched closer and closer to them in the mud.

Very soon there were casualties. Young Green, the officer in charge of our Shropshire digging party, was the first. He was shot through the head and killed. Radford was shot in the head and died shortly afterwards. Very soon about twenty of the Shropshires were hit. The four of our own men who had come up with us had all been hit by some shrapnel as we were coming up Fargate.

I found Schon and we wondered what could best be done. He got some volunteers and went out to try and put up some wire in front of our trench, but the Bosch were much too near and in a minute or two he was hit by a bullet in the head. Fortunately, Scott came along at that moment and took charge of things. We didn't do any more work that night, but cleared out as quickly as we could.

***

Early in the morning in the dugout we were having some rum and bully before going to bed when old Schon appeared. He had a great bandage around his head and was still bleeding pretty hard, but he was quite cheerful. I think he had had some rum at the dressing station just along the bank. It was, to all appearances, quite a light wound and had only just touched the skull. He stayed a few minutes and then went off to the ambulance that had just arrived.

How I missed old Schon after that. I had never realised how much his cheery, placid presence had meant to us. If anything went wrong, it was he who always turned it into a joke and made us see how amusing the whole thing really was. His point of view was always so novel and original. Nothing ever worried him.

***

It was decided by the bigwigs back at division and corps that it was no good trying to get back the remains of the original front line. For one thing it was pounded to bits since the Bosch had occupied it.

On the 20th, Hopkins was ordered to reconnoitre for a new front line which was to link up Wyatt's Lane, S32 and 'Butt 18'. It was a rotten job as no one knew where the Bosch were or how far they had come. That evening he just sniffed, took his old stick and went off with an orderly. I believe, as a matter of fact, he got lost. He never found S32. I don't wonder at it.

21st February 1916

Next day, everything was arranged. I was to take out a big wiring party consisting of half the company and run a line of wire in front of the proposed new front line.

We had a regular drill for wiring. There were definite carrying parties who dumped stakes and wire in a line at intervals. Then came the men who screwed the stakes into the ground and after them the wirers etc.

First of all, there was the covering party of 200 infantry to be placed in position in front to keep off enemy patrols. I started off with them from 'Butt 18'. There were no landmarks and no one knew the country at all. I had to steer entirely by the moon in the direction I thought S32 lay.

The country towards S32 was an appalling swamp. It was flat and low lying and consisted of great ancient shell craters, brim full of water, whose surface was covered with slime and green fungus. You had to thread your way among the craters along the narrow muddy ridges between them.

Here and there a farm must once have stood. There were one or two bricks and a broken cartwheel. In one place was a great heap of English wagons thrown one on top of the other by shells. And there were skeletons of men and horses. This must have been a busy little camp or horse lines before the Second Battle of Ypres. There was one skull with a rag tied round its face. They must have been there ever since that thin green mist rolled over the Pilckem Ridge and overwhelmed them.[57]

By some extraordinary luck, I hit off S32 straight away. The line was now marked out by a row of men and work could be started on the actual wiring. It was very slow work. Half the carrying party didn't turn up with the material till late. It was just freezing and there was a bitter east wind so that the men's fingers were numb with the cold after quite a short time.

There was trouble with the covering party too. There always was trouble with covering parties. They would either keep coming right in on top of the wire or else collecting in groups at the bottoms of the biggest and deepest shell craters they could find. It took us three nights to do that thousand yards of wire[58]. Then we started the worst bit of all, from S32 to Wyatt's Lane.

The first night, 24th February, we didn't get anything done. The whole wiring party was dispersed by shell fire and machine guns. The same thing happened the next night. To make matters worse there was a bright moon, and snow had fallen so that even in our white snow overalls we were spotted and fired on at once. The night after, there was a thaw and the mud became so bad that it was impossible to carry the wiring materials, wire pickets etc. out to the job. The men simply sank in and stuck.

In all, we were on that job and the subsequent work on the new trench behind the wire for eleven nights in succession. Several times we came across Bosch patrols and there were little bombing competitions. Once I met a party of them dressed in British uniforms and was very nearly caught. Another time I lost my way and wandered into E29 on the right. The garrison were very jumpy for the Bosch had been rushing some more posts further on the right and they were seeing forms in the darkness all round them. Before I knew anything I was surrounded with bayonets and wild, strained faces. It was a desperate job to convince them I was genuine.

It was an eerie place, that canal. All the romance of that first sight of it in the moonlight gradually disappeared and a general depression born of constant fear and strain came in its place. Whether it was the dampness of the place and the peculiar atmosphere of the water over the Yperlee, or the continual nocturnal life I don't know, but there was an air of depression and gloom which hung over everybody. It was about the time of the opening of the Bosch offensive at Verdun and I think that there was an idea that a great offensive might take place against us at the same time.

I used to dread that nightly journey up the trench to my work. There was the constant fear of the enfilade gun, which used to knock out whole platoons as they felt their way in the dark along the uneven trench-boards. There was the bridge with Mad Alec playing on it in little, short vicious bursts.

The further to the left one went, the worse the canal seemed to become. The dugouts got fewer and the trench worse and worse. The extreme left, where the Yperlee runs into the canal, was a ghastly place. Here the Bosch were on the opposite bank of the canal, not more than 100 feet away. This was where the trench mortars lived. The Bosch used to throw over immense things that exploded with a deafening noise that could be heard all over the Salient. Once or twice, I saw them in the moonlight from the top of the east bank while going along Fargate: great things like beer barrels, hurtling over the still water of the canal, turning over and over as they went. On the west bank just opposite our own trench, mortars would try and reply. There was a horrible tale of four batteries being wiped out in four days, disappearing into the mud. The last officer fired twenty rounds with his battery and went mad.

Beyond the sluice all was vagueness. The French were there. They seemed to hold no trenches and several times the Bosch came over the canal and raided them. There was apparently nothing to stop them from getting across and attacking us from behind.

The extreme left seemed shrouded in mystery. I never saw it at all by daylight. North of Bridge 6W you couldn't go by day except just along the canal bank gangway and even there, right under cover of the bank it was dangerous to move north of [Bridge] 6D on account of snipers shooting straight down from the Bosch trenches beyond the bend to the north.

One gets strange ideas about a country one has only groped in about at night by moonlight or by the intermittent flickering of individual star shells momentarily lighting up the inky blackness of a rainy night.

Even at night no one walked about in the open behind the canal bank unless his work took him there. The whole country up near the French area at any rate, was swept continuously by at least eight Bosch machine guns from dusk to dawn. As far back as our store done at Belmont Farm, showers of bullets used to come over and we had many horses hit there. Even along the gangway right in under the cover of the canal bank, one was never safe. The Bosch enfilade battery right up the canal would choose a particularly dark night to send volleys of high explosive shells that burst in the air just above you and sent you tripping and stumbling down the broken trench-boards towards the nearest dugout. They seemed alive, those enfilade shells. They'd follow you down the gangway for hundreds of yards in the dark, flashing blinding yellow and reverberating with great metallic crashes from side to side of the hollow of the canal. And when they'd chased you into a dugout, breathless, caked with mud from the side of the bank and bruised with many falls, they seemed to halt and stamp about outside, angrily waiting for you to come out.

I used to dream of the moonlit country up the canal beyond our boundary, the land where those long lines of shattered trees went to. I dreamed of running through the main street of Boesinghe with a crowd of French all with handkerchiefs round their mouths running away from something terrible that was rolling after us.

***

For about a week after Schon was hit, we were very shorthanded in the way of officers. I think I was the only subaltern who was doing anything. Watson was sick with an attack of trench fever and Miers had been hit by a splinter in the foot during the bombardment a couple of days after we had taken over from the 14th Division.

Scott and I lived in the dugout at Bridge 6. What a haven of rest that dugout was when one came in in the early morning just as it was beginning to get light with one's coat stiff with frozen mud so that it stood up when it was taken off, and one's breeches and boots caked with mud. For the first time for about eleven hours you were safe. The enfilade gun could fire up and down the canal bank as much as it liked and you heard the '*tap tap tap*' of Mad Alec away up there, riddling the wretched canvas screen along Bridge 6D without a tremor.

How nice it was to get inside and shut the door and light the candle. The yellow light of the candle was the most beautiful thing after a night out in the snow and sleet and the groping in the dark in the intervals between the old white floating Verey lights that rose and fell again before you could see where you were. How peaceful it was in there with Scott's regular breathing and the '*tap tap tock tock tock*' of the machine gun far away. There was some cold food waiting on the table and best of all there was a bottle of rum, some water and a glass.

You'd drop off to sleep to the dull shuffling of men passing up and down the gangway just outside the dugout door. When you woke up the same sound greeted you. At night the footsteps were slow and uncertain, groping for broken slats in the trench-boards. Sometimes there was just one man. Sometimes a long column in single file. If there was a hole in the trench-boards just outside your door, you'd hear a monotonous repetition of warnings passed back along the line of men: 'Mind the 'ole', ''ole', ''ole' ''ole', 'Mind the 'ole', [and] 'There's an 'ole, 'ere', a pause then a crash and muttered curses as some unfortunate man perhaps carrying a load of rations picked himself up from the slippery track.

***

Life on the canal rarely began before midday. Nearly everyone had been up most of the night before on some job or other. Brigade Headquarters was never busy before twelve and consequently no one else was.

Scott and I generally got up about half past eleven and had a sort of breakfast-lunch at twelve. After that there were various odd jobs to be done, details to be arranged for the evening etc. They usually didn't take long. The rest of the day until dark was free. We generally had tea at half past three and dinner at half past six. At about seven we started off. The section and I, and nearly always an infantry working party, made our way up that long uneven gangway that ran northwards under the shelter of the canal bank. Directly that march started one seemed to drop into another existence, as if one was living two lives.

Those few hours of daylight were awfully precious and had to be made the most of. The day seemed wasted if one sat down and read a book. No, there was a craving to be satisfied, an unconscious one, and that was the company of other people.

It is probably hard for those who haven't lived under similar conditions to realise what joy there was in strolling along to someone else's dugout and having a chat and perhaps a drink. It seemed quite natural to walk into someone's dugout whom you had never seen before and sit down and play his gramophone. There were very few, however, whom we didn't know.

It was a perfect community that canal bank, for the few hours of the day that we knew it. We all lived along one gangway with the long ridge of the bank behind us as a shelter and the dirty little Yperlee stream in front. We got up when we liked, dressed how we liked and did what we liked. You talked to anyone as if you had known him all your life or you didn't talk at all, whichever you felt like. Except that no one ever talked about personal things. We said exactly what we thought and we disliked nobody.

On our left in the immediate neighbourhood of Bridge 6 lived the 84th Field Company, at least Huddleston the OC was there and two sections with him. Everybody liked Huddleston. He was a regular RE captain who had spent most of his time at survey work. He was a great, tall, kind-hearted, humorous fellow and his company worshipped him.

On the right there came first of all the Durhams, the pioneer battalion. They occupied about 200 yards of gangway. We always got on well with the Durhams. You could get three times as much work out of a digging party of their men as you could out of anyone else. Their officers were the jolliest lot. They were always keen on their work and always cheerful, even on the worst of wet nights. The two things I remember about the premises on the canal were their mess with its unceasing gramophone and unlimited whisky bottle, and the barber. There was always the barber right in the middle of the gangway with his chair and apron. When the shells came, the barber would take his chair and his 'patient' and disappear into a dugout.

Further along to the right came a reserve battalion of infantry and after that Brigade Headquarters. There were: 'Old Roy' (the brigadier), Blunt (brigade major), Lionel Tennyson (staff captain), and Brace (brigade signals officer). Beyond that came the battalions of another brigade, the 59th or the 61st.

***

27th February 1916

On the 27th February, the 60th Brigade was relieved by the 61st and the 84th Field Company took over our work on the new front line on the extreme left. I took one of the officers – White – all round in front of S32 and Wyatt's Lane etc. to show him everything. The 60th Brigade went into reserve and rested in the hut camps down the Elverdinghe road towards Poperinghe.

We were now the Reserve Field Company and gave up all work in front of the canal. Hopkins and Scott went back to our camp at Dromore Corner and I took over the work the 84th [Field Company] had been doing on the canal bank with my section and Schon's old section (No. 2). The work was chiefly the maintenance of the bridges and the construction of new dugouts on the canal bank. That very day, the two main bridges on the left ([Bridge] 6D and [Bridge] 6W) were shelled down and had to be repaired before the nightly procession of ration parties and reliefs could proceed up towards the front line across the canal.

Next day, a new officer, Second Lieutenant Smith by name, arrived to take Schon's place. He was sent up to take over No. 2 Section and to help me. We shared the bridges between us. He was a Scotchman [*sic*], rather short and very unassuming, an electrical engineer from Edinburgh. We shared the dugout just south of Bridge 6.

It was nice being left alone up there with Hopkins and Scott away back at the camp. We got on very well. Rations used to come up each night on a limber and they sent us up whisky and food from the main mess for our little mess. Verhoustraten saw to that. He was very good at looking after us in the way of food for the mess.

Our chief work was the maintenance of the bridges from Bridge 4 to the end on the left. We organised maintenance parties who were always in readiness with little dumps of bridging material at various points along the bank. Then there were bridge patrols who inspected every bridge three times a day and reported any breakdowns to me. The only time one could repair bad breakdowns, which generally happened during the day, was immediately it got dark. There was always a rush to get a bridge through before the heavy forward traffic of working parties etc. started. If there was a bad gap on a battalion relief night, there would be company after company waiting impatiently in the cold to get across. Colonels would come up and grumble. Bridge 6D was the worst. It was the last bridge on the left and fed the whole of the front line on the extreme left, right up to Wyatt's Lane. It was under daytime observation by the Bosch, who were now up at the bend in our old trenches at F35, and it was shelled down regularly. At dusk our repair parties had to work right out in the middle, 10 feet above the canal, with Mad Alec traversing backwards and forwards in little sharp bursts of half a dozen rounds or so. That machine gunner was a humourist as well as an expert gunner. He would tap out tunes on his gun, which is very hard to do. He would go 'Ti-tiddly-i-ti-pom-pom' right down the middle of the canal.

We were also responsible for maintaining the charges of guncotton on all the bridges and the electric cables and alternative instantaneous fuses running back to the bank so that in case of emergency, all communication across the canal could be cut without an instant's delay. This meant other maintenance parties had to go round testing the circuits and replacing the charges that often got knocked away by shrapnel splinters. My Lance Corporal Wilson was the head of this department. He was mad keen on explosives and was the section expert.

There were a lot of other odd jobs as well. Smith started work on a new low-level bridge with the tops of the piles totally submerged and the planking etc. stowed away on the bank, ready to be run out at any time. We wanted a bridge that the Bosch didn't know anything about.

On the 6th March, there was more wind up[59] about the activity of the Bosch and the frequent raids across the canal into the French area. Just opposite Wyatt's Lane was Bridge 7Z, which until the night of 12th February had been used regularly to communicate with the front line garrison in the original line F35, F34 etc. It was a well-built bridge of heavy crib piers and was intact, although of course quite unusable owing to the Bosch being so close.

Sometime before, Ward of the 84th Field Company had a go at demolishing it. He managed to get a charge of guncotton out by crawling along in the dark intervals between the Verey lights and put a sandbag over it to keep it in place. When the next light went up, the old Bosch spotted something lying there and riddled it with machine gun bullets for about a quarter of an hour on end. The 84th [Field Company] succeeded in blocking up the end of the bridge with barbed wire, but no one after that episode liked to go out and put any more charges on the bridge.

However, it had to be done somehow. We made long narrow wooden boxes with about 40 pounds of guncotton in each and intended to float them across the canal at the feet of the piers. This didn't work as the whole place was full of floating debris and wreckage. At last, we made a rush for it and got 80 pounds of guncotton on to the top of the first pier some way out over the water, by carrying them out on the bridge itself. Of course, a flare went up just as we were right out in the open on the bridge. 'Heavens they must have seen us.' There was snow on the bridge and on the banks and we were only about 50 yards off them. By some extraordinary luck they didn't. We scrambled back to the bank and loosed off the charge with a fine old crash. Two complete bays were destroyed, and we left it at that.

***

7th March 1916

Next day, the 7th, my section was relieved by No. 3 under a new officer, a South African named Hands, aged about 24. We marched back that evening down the Essex Farm road and along the main Brielen–Elverdinghe road to Elverdinghe and thence down to our camp at Dromore Corner – a little section of about thirty men and a tool cart, sandwiched in amongst the continuous double column of ration wagons, ammunition limbers, water carts and relieving troops that crawled along all the roads just after dark and filled the air with an uninterrupted, subdued noise of thousands of cartwheels and horses' hoofs moving slowly along the *pavé* roads.

For the next few days, we had a good rest, being employed only in camp. There were the company workshops – sawmill and carpenter's shops etc. – to be looked after, stores to be drawn from the CRE's yard down the road just by Steentje Mill and the stables for the horses to be finished.

One of the first things to do was to go to the field cashier and get some money. He used to appear from nowhere in the vague background of Corps Headquarters in a great motor car at stated intervals and places in the 'forward area' as he called it. His nearest meeting place for us was Viulle Seule Cabaret.

The field cashier was a kind of institution. There was always a crowd of officers there waiting for him. He was invariably late. One met one's friends there and groused about 'those damned people who roll about right back at Corps in motor cars. They might at least turn up on time.'

***

Our little mess in the farm consisted of Hopkins, the Belgian interpreter Verhoustraten, and myself. Scott was on leave, I think. Sometimes Massey, the Adjutant, or the CRE would drop in from Divisional Headquarters in the hut camp they'd made for themselves down the Elverdinghe Road, just beyond the mill.

Verhoustraten was an amusing fellow, aged about 28. He had been a bank clerk in Antwerp before the war. He had a funny old horse called Bessie on which he used to jog off rather unsteadily into Poperinghe to buy things for the mess. He was, of course, mess secretary – what's the use of an interpreter if not to run one's mess? He never did anything else. His proposals for the day's work were always the same: 'In t'morning I go on Bessie by Poperinghe. In t'afternoon I go again on Bessie by Poperinghe.' He used to have vague, disjointed stories of the beginning of the war. He was apparently a ragtime volunteer in the Belgian artillery until they lost their guns by their being put in a different train which went in another direction. Then, we gathered, he became a sort of anti-aircraft guard and fired a revolver at aeroplanes from the roof of a hotel in Ostend. He always gave one the impression of being a harmless, innocent spectator at a rough game he didn't understand, swept in amongst the players, pushed about dizzily for a short time, and then thrown out again.

Hopkins' moroseness in the mess was getting to be a great trial. Ever since he came into the area, he was very much worse. He never spoke except to grumble about the food. Poor chap, we didn't understand it at the time, but it was because of the trouble with the brigadier. He had done him out of his promotion by an adverse report. He used to curse Hopkins whenever he saw him. Roy seemed, to the majority of us, to be going off his head. Blunt, the brigade major, was doing all the work at the brigade office while Roy just interfered.

10th March 1916

On the 10th, three days after we had come back from the canal, work started again. This time it meant marching or riding up almost to the canal every night from the camp, about 4 miles.

There was trouble with the traffic on the Essex Farm road. Everything – rations, RE stores etc. – had to be taken up to the canal by that road for the whole division. There had been a series of bad 'road straffs' at night, in which men, horses and wagons had been knocked out as they stood in a column by the road, by bursts of shelling.

The idea was to put the Windsor Castle tramway into working order so that supplies for the left brigade could be off loaded at Mordacq crossroads and pushed up to the canal on trucks. At the time, the little tramway – an ordinary, 19-inch-gauge trench tramway affair – was in a bad state. It was made of wooden rails that had been there some time and were rotting. It had to be replaced by a steel track all the way and the trucks had to be overhauled and renewed.

My section and a platoon of the Durhams were detailed for the job. We were always glad to get a Durham working party. It meant that the job would get on three times as quickly as with anybody else. I was always rather fond of working on trench tramways and was more or less looking forward to it.

For the first few nights the Bosch kept quiet. Then the trouble started. The area was full of spies and the Bosch got wind of a change in the transport arrangements at night. (There were strange officers seen in various places in the Salient about this time. They were supposed to have walked in either through the gap in the line between S32 and E29, or to have come across from the French area. One was actually caught on the canal bank. One was almost caught at Elverdinghe by a Durham sentry but managed to escape.) Salvos of shells used to arrive at Dawson's Corner, just as a column of traffic came past. There were stories of a rocket going up from the woods and bursts of shelling answering it.

Whatever the cause, the shelling of the roads at night, especially at the junction of Dawson's Corner and Mordacq Road, became very bad. There would be furious bursts of shelling for a few minutes then quiet for irregular intervals: perhaps ten minutes, perhaps an hour. You rode up each night with your section in a pontoon wagon, knowing that there was practically no chance of getting up to the work in peace without that sinking feeling of terror and anxiety when you see faint little flickers – very faint – in the east and wait ages for the rushing chorus of shells that gets momentarily louder and fiercer, until with a series of blinding flashes they burst all around you, lighting up the road with its crouching men and stampeding horses. The worst part of the journey was when you saw the road ahead being shelled and had to drive on as if you hadn't seen it.

I usually met Stubbs and his platoon of DLI[60] at our store dump at Belmont Farm. We'd load up what stores (rails etc.) we wanted and push them off in trucks to the place where we were working.

Once when I was waiting for him there, I saw a curious sight. There was a dog wandering about and sniffing in the hedge by the side of the road. Suddenly two gigantic rats came out and deliberately attacked him, sending him away hurriedly with his tail between his legs.

Oh! Those rats. Never have there been rats of such a size. There must have been something about the environment of the canal. They were big out of all reason. The 96th Field Company caught one that measured 23 inches from nose to tail. You'd see them in the moonlight, swimming across the canal like a fleet of boats. They fed on the dead out in front.

I think it was these monstrous rats that gave the finishing touches to the unnatural atmosphere of terror and gloom hanging about the canal and about the vague, mysterious outlines of ruined farms hidden in clumps of poplars: thin, leafless trees that threw great skeleton shadows in the moonlight across the stagnant half luminous water of the moat-like ponds.

Towards the end of March, we began to get very stale. We never felt well. There was a certain amount of dysentery about, and an unpleasant complaint known as 'canal throat'. Hands had it badly. We began to look ahead and we saw no end to things. We would go on night after night until a shell came nearer than usual, and one by one we should go to the rapidly growing cemetery behind the canal bank near Bridge 4 where the rest of the division seemed to be going to in a continuous stream of stretchers. Except for the few days at the beginning of February, there had been no real fighting and yet there had been nearly 9,000 casualties since the division came into the area.

***

While I was on leave (29th March–14th April 1916), two things happened. Huddleston the OC of the 84th Field Company was killed by one of our own machine-gunners while reconnoitring out in front of the line at night. It was his own fault for not warning the garrison that he was going out, but there it was. He was a great loss to everybody. He was one of the very best of men. Scott went to take his place as OC 84th Field Company and Lieutenant White came to us as second in command.

White was a temporary officer about 45 years old, who had spent most of his life in South Africa as an architect. We didn't get on with him very well for some reason. He was very obstinate and was always on the buck about what he did in the German East African show before he came to France. However, he was a pleasant enough fellow.

The second thing was that the long-expected infernal machine arrived on the railway. It was a 12-inch howitzer and sat in our horse lines to poop off [*sic*]. It had a little camouflage hut round the truck and the first time it fired they didn't lift enough of the roof off so that it blew the whole hut flat with the blast. Incidentally, it knocked all our mess gear off the shelf in the mess hut.

Up to now we had been very free from shelling back at the camp, except for the first night we arrived there. They occasionally used to shell Divisional Headquarters some way behind and we could hear the 'Pop Gun' in the evenings and the whine of its shells very high up, going over our heads into Poperinghe. Now there was bound to be trouble sooner or later. The day I came back, the Bosch started searching vaguely in the fields with 4.2s. He didn't come very near though.

***

Leave arrangements never were any too comfortable. At that time, the leave train used to start at 1.00 am from Poperinghe Station. I drove down the long *pavé* road into Poperinghe in a limber – without springs – and waited in the train. There was always a certain amount of interest in waiting for the thing to start. It might go any time, so that you couldn't go far away. Also, the Bosch had a playful habit of taking long-range shots at the station with the 'Pop Gun' just about that time of night. One generally got to St Omer at about 6.00 am and wandered on to Boulogne by Calais, getting in some time in the afternoon. The boat never took the slightest interest in the leave train and went at odd times that varied from day to day. Generally, it managed to get away just before the leave train got in so that everybody had to wait for the next one.

14th April 1916

I brought a gramophone back with me on 6th April. Hopkins had a bad liver when I arrived and said that he could never stand the thing for an instant. However, I went straight to the canal to join Smith and White and we worked the gramophone to our hearts' content.

Everyone was brightening up a lot. There were strong rumours of our being relieved by the 6th Division. The weather was good too.

It was a few days after I came back, I remember, that Smith and I paid our first visit to Ypres. We went along the canal bank to the Dead End, past a battalion of the Guards Division who lived along the east bank near the Dead End and up Rue Dixmude. There was a 4.5-inch howitzer sitting in a front room in one of the houses near the Dead End. It didn't see us coming along the road and pooped off just as we were going past. We didn't get very far. The Bosch began putting a few shells over into the town and we got alarmed and turned back. Smith had just been badly shaken up by a whiz-bang[61] that burst almost in his face outside our dugout on the canal bank and blackened his teeth with the explosion; his nerves weren't up to much just then in consequence. It is curious how frightened one gets when there is the slightest danger, if one is merely sightseeing. It's partly because you feel that there is no need for you to be there, and that you were a fool for ever coming, and partly because you are in a place that you don't know the habits of – that you don't understand.

***

The relief began on the 16th April and took several days. An officer from the 2nd/2nd West Riding Field Company of the 6th Division, Lieutenant Chamberlain, arrived on the 14th [April] and lived with us, going over the various jobs we were doing. There was some muddle I believe because on the 16th [April] some officers of the 12th Field Company also arrived and began to take over.

The 6th Division regarded itself as an integral part of the Salient. They had been up there since April 1915 – over a year. During the Second Battle of Ypres, they had been at Armentières, coming up afterwards to relieve the remains of the divisions in front of Ypres and there they had stayed, through all the fighting in the summer and autumn of 1915. They had been on our right (in the right sector of the 14th Corps front, from Weiltje to Hooge) for the first month that we were on the canal bank and were then relieved by the Guards.

They had tales and traditions of every street and crossroads in Ypres: of the 17-inch howitzer of Hellfire Corner, of Hooge and the Menin Road, Hill 60, St Éloi, The Bluff, and all the scores of famous and awe-inspiring spots around the Salient of Ypres. The traditions of Ypres were always passed on from division to division like this. New traditions were continually being added and the old ones carefully preserved in a halo of legend.

***

On the 17th April, we were clear of the canal and its surroundings and marching back through Poperinghe to Winnezeele. We were just out of the camp in time. That day the Bosch found the old 12-inch howitzer and the 12th Field Company were very miserable. The howitzer itself was hit and badly damaged, the stables and workshops were burnt and the whole camp turned upside down. We heard with some amusement that the 12th Field Company had to spend the whole night crouching in some muddy old trenches nearby.

Chapter 3

CALAIS (APRIL–MAY 1916)

We got to Winnezeele in the afternoon of the 18th April after a cold and wet march of about 15 miles. The sections were billeted in four farms near the windmill just east of the village. It didn't take long to settle in – about an hour. Then we went to look for our own billets and our mess.

There was a delightful feeling of freedom and irresponsibility at the end of a day's march after the company was comfortably settled in and the horses and mules picketed. It was so nice to look forward to dinner and know there was nothing to do afterwards. How quiet and peaceful everything was. There were the church bells going and the villagers lounging about; the rattle of a harrow being dragged home by a stolid old farm horse. There was nothing to do – no worries, no machine guns. We were at the beginning of a month's holiday and rest.

We shared the accommodation in the village with the 96th Field Company and the 20th Battalion of the KRRs. We all managed to fit in.

Winnezeele was a typical little village in that part of the country. It consisted of a crossroads with little houses stretching out along the four roads for a few hundred yards, a large cheap church and one or two decent houses. There were three or four estaminets, an épicerie, a brewery and a large repair shop for agricultural machinery, of which there were all sorts in the road outside. There was also a superior estaminet which aspired to a notice, hand-written 'Officers Only'.

The population in the Hazebrouck/Cassel districts, right down to the south of the River Lys, lives in the farms dotted about the country like flies on a flypaper. The villages are only sheer necessities, places to buy things and to go to church on Sundays. There was never any accommodation for troops in the villages themselves, but each farm would hold 100 to 200 men in its barns.

That night we all had a great and noisy time in The Merry Widow pub opposite the church. There was Major Storey the OC of the 96th Field Company and a couple of his subalterns; also White, Smith, Watson and myself, and several of the KRR officers.

The 20th KRR were a battalion that had been rushed out from England half armed and a quarter trained. They were intended for a pioneer battalion, but hadn't been taught anything about trench digging, dugout building or anything. For the next week we set to work to teach them. We got them to dig model trenches in a field, to make breastworks above ground, to lay duckboards on pickets driven into the bottom of the trench, and all the 101 little details of the art of making a habitable trench that wouldn't fall in or get muddy. Then there were model listening posts and saps out in no man's land and wire entanglements of all kinds. Each of our sections took a company of them in hand and we had competitions between the companies in digging and in the speed of constructing wire entanglements. The afternoons we had to ourselves and went for rides out into the country round.

The greatest surprise to us was Hopkins. He was a changed man. He didn't grumble about the food and he shared our jokes and fun in the mess. He even tolerated the gramophone. I think it was the news that General Roy was going that did it.

***

On the 23rd April, Hopkins came in with the news that the 60th Brigade and the attached units – ourselves, the field ambulance etc. were going to Calais for ten days. Cavan was sending the 20th Division off for a holiday by the sea. There was also the news that the old CRE was going and we were getting a younger man. Hopkins, being the senior field company commander, went off to Divisional HQ to act as CRE temporarily.

26th April 1916

We marched to Hopoutre Siding just west of Poperinghe in the afternoon of the 26th April to entrain. Entraining a unit is great fun, especially at night. We got out our old acetylene searchlights and lit up the siding with them. There were no platforms and only three portable ramps with which to get our eighty-odd horses and mules and our fourteen heavy wagons into the train. We had an awful job with the three pontoon wagons, which weigh 3.5 tons each. We got through in an hour and a half and were quite pleased with ourselves at the speed.

From the first day we arrived in Calais we became different people. Life was worth living after all. As we lay basking in the sun outside the mess tent, we could almost feel the damp, unhealthy atmosphere of the last two months being sucked out of us. There wasn't a cloud in the sky and the sun blazed down and glared on the white sand around our tents. What weather it was!

We had no duties to speak of, no work and no worries. We discovered the sea and its potentialities for collective enjoyment. The sea was the great thing. The whole company descended on the sea every morning – men, horses and mules and a wagon with provisions for the midday meal. There were mule races on the sands and games of all kinds, always ending in everybody, animals included, wallowing in the water. It was extraordinary how warm the water was for the time of year.

Beaumaris Camp, where the brigade group lived, consisted of hundreds of bell tents pitched in the loose sand on the high ground about 2 miles from the sea and three from Calais town. The dunes begin about a mile from the camp and run in two great ridges parallel to the sea, between which lies a kind of lagoon bordered with all kinds of sand scrub and gorse.

Each afternoon the brigade was turned loose and about 4,000 officers and men wandered off into Calais. Calais is a poor place at the best of times. Still, it was a proper town and had trams that really worked, and there were restaurants and pubs. Sometimes we dined in the town at The Continental and sometimes we went back to camp for mess. There was usually something doing in the camp after mess in the evening; one of the battalions would get up a concert or something.

***

4th May 1916

On the 4th May, the brigade got up a sports meeting on the sands. Hobart, the new Brigade Major and Lionel Tennyson ran it. Everyone had a great time. The 83rd came off very well. We won the 'wrestling on mules' and several other collective things, but Smith was the star turn with his little white pony. He carried off more than half the mounted events.

Hopkins was there with the red divisional staff armband as CRE, and most of the divisional staff including the GOC, General Douglas Smith.

Hopkins was beaming all over and being quite a societal success! Roy was all smiles too. The old man was making himself pleasant the last few days before leaving the brigade.

The only unfortunate incident in the day occurred on the way home. My horse Billy was always a bit mad, and inclined to bolt, and that afternoon all the horses were very excited after the racing. He bolted, and Watson's horse who was alongside also bolted. We swept down the road at rest, clearing everything before us. Things went well for the first mile, and then we came to a T-junction with a barbed wire fence in front. My mind became a blank for a second or two as we went straight through the wire with hardly a stumble and pulled up in a ploughed field. Watson for some reason had tried to turn and brought his horse down with a crash on the stone pavement. We stopped a passing car and took him off to the hospital in the casino with concussion and a head, the size of a football. The horse was in an awful mess and had to be shot. Billy, however, had smashed the 4-foot-wire fence down and hadn't even a scratch!

***

5th May 1916

Next day, the 5th May, I left by train for Herzeele with a small advance party to take over the billets of the 84th Field Company, and to look over the work they were doing on the L Line between Brielen and Vlamertinghe. The rest of the Company left Calais on the 6th [May] on foot with the brigade, doing the odd 50 miles in a three-day track. Of course, the orders were altered, and they didn't fetch up at Herzeele after all. I found them at Ledeghem a couple of miles south of Esquelbecque where Division HQ was.

Hopkins returned to the Company on the 8th [May], the new CRE having arrived. He was Colonel Holland RE who had come from the 55th Field Company of the Guards Division, and was reported to be a very good chap.

Just before we left Calais, our great and lasting acquisition arrived – the new brigade commander, Brigadier Butler. He also came from the Guards Division and had been commanding the 2nd Irish Guards. What a change from the last one. He was a tall, middle-aged man with golden hair and a fresh, pink face, very quiet and imperturbable and with a kind word for everybody. The spirit of a Kitchener's Army Brigade immediately. There was no guardsman's insistence on 'spit and polish'.

He never had brigade inspections and things, and yet the discipline was as good as one could wish. He was one of the two or three personalities who made the division into the best fighting division in the Battle of the Somme.

***

Our company had two new officers while we were at Calais. Second Lieutenant H.Y.V. Jackson arrived at Beaumaris Camp on the same day as we did. He was a little short fellow, about 27, who had enlisted as a sapper in the Royal Naval Division and had been wounded in the stomach at Gallipoli. He was an electrical engineer in Westinghouse's. He came to take Hands' place (who had been evacuated with trench foot) just before we left the canal.

Then while we were at Ledeghem, Holgate arrived. He was a South African, about 24, and had been through the German West African show as a trooper. He and White soon started quarrelling. It was a great blow for White who now couldn't buck about things at all, as Holgate always used to corroborate his statements and assumed the standpoint that White had never seen anything of the fighting in German SW at all. It was screamingly funny. The two used to go at each other hammer and tongs. We always took Holgate's side.

11th May 1916

On 11th May, Holgate and I – with our sections – went up by bus to take over the work that the 84th [Field Company] were doing in the L Line. Scott and half his company were living in Machine-Gun Farm, just south of Brielen with two companies of the Durhams.

We had a very jolly time therefore the next ten days. We were absolutely on our own, being on detached duty and working directly under the Chief Engineer of the 14th Corps. At least, we got stores and things from the CE's stores officer. We never saw or heard from the CE's people otherwise. I had about 200 infantry attached for work. They lived in dugouts around the place.

The L Line consisted of breastwork[62] posts at L2 Wood, Brielen, Machine-Gun Farm, Reigersburg and L4 near the railway crossing on the main road. There was an enormous amount of work to be done on them. Like everything else, they had been allowed to collapse and fall into decay.

None of us overworked. We rather felt that we had been done out of part of our holiday. We were about ten in the mess in the farm, which at that time was almost intact. The Durhams really were a wonderful crowd. There were some real characters among them. One of them was the leading Harrogate dentist, another was a big cigarette manufacturer. Stubbs, my old companion of the railway building was there too. We all had a thoroughly good time.

***

There was another new officer there too, up from the New Army right down south. There had been vague rumours about preparations somewhere in the south. Extraordinary rumours. This fellow had stories of line upon line of gun positions, of great railway sidings being built and of columns of huge guns crawling along the roads at night. We didn't believe much of it. However, there had been rumours of divisions disappearing one by one from the old British front in the north and vaguely 'going south'.

Our ideas of the war as a whole were very vague. I knew what divisions were holding the various parts of the line down as far as Neuve Chapelle, that the British front went down as far as Loos where the French line started. Beyond that we knew that there was a British Third Army somewhere by Albert and then nothing but rumours.

The British Army was becoming so vast, one couldn't visualise the whole of it. The army we were part of (Plumber's Second Army) was all we were interested in, and it had nine divisions like our own, each of which would take up 14 miles of roadway when on the march: 114 miles of roadway altogether! And yet there were three British armies like that, and now rumours of a fourth and even a fifth forming down there in the south. Sometimes we used to speculate on future battles and operations. The great German attack on Verdun was still going on, but it was so far away it didn't interest us. We knew so little, so the larger aspect of the war was not worth taking much notice of. Our division would go where fate decreed. Sooner or later we felt we were bound to be drawn into the great whirlpool that was gathering in the south. When didn't matter and our fate was so uncertain that it was no good thinking about it. Everything was so far beyond us.

There was never any serious thought of the war ending. It had long since become a habit, a permanent form of existence, the general average of which was not altogether unpleasant. The contrast between happiness and trouble was infinitely greater than at home, that was all. The mean value remained the same.

As for the immediate prospect, if things went on normally, we should relieve the Guards Division in front of Ypres in a short time. There was nothing to interrupt the regular rotation of the three divisions of the 14th Corps: the Guards, the 6th [Division] and ourselves. Two divisions would hold the line and the third be out resting in the back areas: two months in the line and a month out.

We were going up to the most famous area in the old British front. All the romance of Ypres and the longing to be there was coming back. What must the War have been like to the people who could feel no spark of the wonderful romance of it, the romance that made one want to go to places that were famous through the fear of them.

Chapter 4

YPRES (MAY–JULY 1916)

18th May 1916

Holgate and I rejoined the company at Winnezeele on the 17th May and next morning Hopkins, Jackson and I rode up to meet the 76th Field Company of the Guards Division whom we were relieving.

The 76th [Field Company] were living partly at a hop store on the main road just behind Vlamertinghe and partly in huts in A30 Wood north-east of Brandhoek.

It was a glorious day, but terribly hot. The dust and petrol vapour hung in a great thick cloud along the main road and there wasn't a breath of wind. We were nearly dead by the time we got to A30 Wood, but it only made the shade and cool of the wood all the nicer. It was the usual kind of wood with young oak trees and undergrowth of hazel, but very much larger than any other in the neighbourhood. At this time of year it was looking lovely. The trees were just coming out and there were ferns and bluebells about. Neat little groups of huts were dotted about here and there – the new Divisional Headquarters Camp that the Prince of Wales (then Q2, 14th Corps) had just put up.

We soon discovered that this was too good for us to live in. [The] 20th Divisional HQ rolled up in a car in the shape of a red-tabbed major and claimed the whole place.

It was arranged that we should go down to the hop store on the main road and have our horse lines in a farm just south of Brandhoek in square G12.

***

The hop store was quite a good place. It was a three-storey building in which there was ample room for the whole company plus workshops and stores. We only occupied the first and ground floors, however, as there was already a small shell-hole in the roof, and the place was right on the main road, which hadn't got a reputation for freedom from shelling. The 76th [Field Company] had their officers' quarters and mess there too, in an estaminet adjoining, but this has been blown up and burnt by a chance shell a couple of weeks before. No one had been hurt but the OC had lost all his kit and got a fortnight's leave to England on the strength of having to buy some more.

Hopkins left us to take over all the billets and stores etc at the hop store and went on up to Ypres to see the OC 76th [Field Company] who was living there with two sections of his company.

As we marched up the Main Road, the *Voie Sacrée* of the British Army, just after dusk the following night, the war seemed to take on a different aspect altogether from that of the last dismal sector to the north. All the excitement and the romance of the Front came rushing back just when we thought it was dead. The damp, misty winter was gone. The trees were all out and there was the smell of long grass growing rankly in the dew of the evening in the neglected fields on either side. The thick avenue of trees shut in the heat and dust of the day like a tunnel, with holes here and there where the moon shone through and lit up little patches on the road.

It was the German boast that those who marched up that road into Ypres never returned, but this didn't worry anybody in the slightest. Every foreboding was forgotten in the wonderful idea that not only was this the most famous place of the time, but the cause of its fame was actually existing. It was *being* famous.

I kept forming mental pictures of scenes in the history of the road to Ypres. First there came the small patrols of Uhlans at the very beginning of the war, then the arrival of the British from the south-west, followed by the precarious days of the First Battle of Ypres with the first refugees, the well to do, driving back in carriages and motors. These were all the owners of the great country houses around. Hopkins had seen the last train steaming out of Ypres station in October 1914.

Then came the terrible days of April and May 1915. The great gas attack and the bombardment of Ypres, when the flames of the burning town lit up almost the whole of Flanders. I pictured the chaos and confusion on the main road at night, the reinforcements and ambulances struggling up against the tide of half-gassed stragglers from Langemark, and terrified refugees from Ypres carrying all their worldly belongings. Wagons and cars ditched in the mud, long-range shells wining overhead, the whole country lit up by the red glare of the flames of the burning city, and every few minutes the ground quaking with the detonation of a 17-inch shell somewhere among the ruins.

Then came the shell shortage when men marched up to hold impossible trenches in the new line into which the Germans had forced them. Trenches down below the ridge and circling Ypres, in which the enemy could observe everything that went on: any little act of hostility – a bomb thrown or a shell fired – entailed prompt punishment from the enemy in the form of a heavy bombardment that lasted for hours. And they knew we could not reply.

I thought of all the friends I knew at school who had marched up this road and been killed in front of Ypres. The last had been Grindley – killed in a wiring party in front of Railway Wood in November last year. One by one we passed the spots we had heard the other division talk about – Goldfish Château, the railway crossing, the asylum, the bridge over the 'Dry Switch' (the dry Ypres–Comines canal) and then Ypres itself with its long streets of clean-swept *pavé* and roofless houses.

***

The 60th Brigade to which the 83rd Field Company was still affiliated was taking over (from the Second Guards Brigade) the sector of the front a thousand yards on either side of the Ypres–Roulers railway. Our left extended to the end of the Ypres–Potijze road, where the 59th Brigade began, and extended to Morteltje ('Mortality') Estaminet. Our right flank ended in a gap in the line just north of Hooge.

The company was split up as follows. Hopkins, Smith, Jackson and I with our sections lived in Ypres, while White and Verhoustraten, the headquarters personnel, workshops etc. and Holgate's section were back at Vlamertinghe. Of the three sections forward, Jackson had charge of the work in the left half of the brigade sector – from a line drawn from the Menin Gate to Railway Wood on the right to the Potijze Road on the left. My section had the right half, bounded by the Menin Road on the right. This was the southern boundary of the 14th Corps and next door to us were the Canadians.

Smith's section was engaged on work in Ypres, such as water supply, concrete machine-gun emplacements in the town, and draining and strengthening cellars to extend the accommodation.

***

The great feature of the Salient was the fact that it lay in a hollow surrounded, except westwards, by a continuous semicircular ridge of about 2 miles radius the whole of which was held by the Germans. From the heights by Hill 60 in the south-east and from the Wytschaete Ridge in the south, they overlooked every bit of ground to the south of the main road as far back as Vlamertinghe, so that no traffic could get into Ypres except at night. From the higher ground above Hooge they could look right down the Menin Road as far as the corner by the *école*. Over the trees round White Château and Pink Château they could watch the tall, jagged fingers of the churches and buildings of Ypres slowly crumbling away month after month under their howitzer fire. Everything to the north and north-west was overlooked by the Pilckem Ridge, which stretched up to the flooded area opposite the French and Belgians along the Yser. Only in Ypres, surrounded by the old ramparts, was there any cover from view.

It is difficult to give any idea of the vital importance of the configuration of the ground in our lives. It affected our whole existence and way of living. All our work was in the earth. It was the one great idea in our minds, to battle with the loose, collapsing earth and the mud at the bottoms of the trenches. On the lie of the ground depended where we lived, and whether we worked by night or day; whether the line was comfortable or uncomfortable.

I was lucky in my little sector. The ground rose fairly steeply up to the front line in Railway Wood and then flattened off, so that for a hundred yards or so behind, one was not under direct observation. Excepting that there was always the danger of whiz-bangs, one could walk about on Cambridge Road in the open daylight. One could get up to and along the front line fairly easily by day too. In Jackson's sector, on the other hand, there was nothing doing in daytime at all. You couldn't even get there. The communication trenches weren't good enough to conceal you from the Bosch who sniped you with field guns instead of the accustomed and familiar rifle – a peculiarity of the Salient.

***

Railway Wood was an important point. (The wood has long ago disappeared). It was one of the only bits of high ground we had. Although not a hilltop, it was at the end of a spur that runs from the main bridge by Zonnebeeke behind the German lines. It had been captured by the British in a terribly costly attack in the summer of 1915, the old line along Cambridge Road having been found impossible as the Bosch could look down into the bottoms of the trenches.

Shortly after the capture of Railway Wood, the 117th Tunnelling Company arrived on the scene, and began a weird subterranean war of their own quite unconnected with what was happening on the surface. They worked on their own and took no orders from anyone except from [British] Army Headquarters, from a mysterious controller of mines.

Under Railway Wood, within a hundred yards or so of the Bosch front line, they had now a system of tunnel dugouts to hold several hundred men, right down in the blue clay. Here they lived month after month while division relieved division and corps relieved corps on the surface above. From these dugouts ran a huge system of shafts and galleries on three separate levels spreading out under the front line and out under no man's land from the railway to the Bellewaardebeek.

Now and then, once a fortnight or so, a mine would be blown, sometimes a big one that made a great crater in no man's land or under the Bosch line. Sometimes a camouflet or little mine exploded deep down in the ground to destroy galleries of the opposing side. Sometimes detachments would get cut off at the end of a sap and die of suffocation or starvation.

The whole of no man's land in this sector was just a series of great craters, some 120 feet across, and Railway Wood was transformed into a huge heap of dark blue-grey clay and decaying sandbags.

I met Dalgas first one evening after dark at Hellfire Corner a few days after our arrival. A little, short man with rather long arms and huge eyes shining out of a black silhouette of a face, hurrying past in the dark. He warned me in a curious foreign accent not to go up the railway as there was a fixed rifle firing down it and his orderly had been shot through the head while by his side.

I thought it must be he – the Guards Division RE had told us stories about him. The man with the 'German' accent[63] who appeared and disappeared through his tunnels unexpectedly and kept getting arrested by new infantry units as they took over the trenches above. Later on in the night I passed a hole in the side of a trench, with the stairs going down into the grey clay whence issued a smell combining good food cooking with stale humanity. I went down.

They had a tiny mess down there, just not high enough to stand upright in and about 6 feet square. There was a bench all round and a square table in the middle so that there was just room to sit. There were eight officers there, mostly of the 20th Division, who had come there for the first time like myself. As I appeared at the entrance, they all moved up one place and made room for me at the corner. 'Hullo', said Dalgas. 'Here's another of them. Whole division'll be here soon. Have a drink, God-damn-it! Pass the whisky along, James.'

He was asking all about our division and telling stories about all the other divisions who had come and gone. Every few minutes a grimy head would appear in the doorway and a corporal in clay-caked overalls would come to report:

> Everything alright in No. 43, sir' or 'Sapper 'ardy's still up at the end of No. 12, sir. 'asn't 'eard anything for two hours. I couldn't 'ear nothing either, sir. I don't like it.

Presently, Fisher, the brigade trench mortar officer, came in and we all moved around another place and everybody had to have another drink. There was no chance of getting out until one had worked one's way right around the table to the door again.

It was like discovering another world down underground. Here was this Danish Subaltern with the big eyes and jerky, guttural voice, carrying on a war of his own, making offensives of his own and parrying Bosch thrusts in the clay all along the front north of Hooge. Down underneath the deep gallery we were sitting in, the ground was full of his men. Solitary listeners sitting at the ends of long saps right out under no man's land; parties working at the faces of new galleries; gangs of men pumping out the water; gangs of men at the air pumps; more men pushing tiny trucks along the narrow galleries piled up with bags of clay; surface men hauling up the bags and carrying them off.

'Outside people' were always welcome and there was a meal and a drink waiting for anyone who cared to drop in at any time, night or day. Dalgas was always there. He never seemed to sleep. One was invariably greeted with the old remark, 'Have a drink, God-damn-it!' I've never seen anything like such hospitality. Nearly always the little dugout was full of a cheerful crowd of officers. The grim, stately Hopkins was enticed in there one night on his way round the line. It was talked of four days afterwards. Dalgas kept him there for an hour and made him talk as he'd never done before.

***

About this time, the 25th May, the chief centre of interest in the brigade was at the two mine craters at H18. The Bosch was observed to be running an open sap out from his front line towards them. The sap stopped about 25 yards off and in a day or two, the familiar blue sandbags appeared, indicating that some deep digging was going on in the blue clay subsoil.

Then the mine scares began. Nothing unsettles a garrison of the front line more than rumours of enemy mines underneath them. The infantry began to hear noises in the ground in every fire bay. They dug holes and got into them to listen.

The immediate fear was that the Bosch would run a sap out underground to the edge of our craters, blow up the front lips of them, and then rush them with an infantry party. If the Bosch once got those craters, our hold on Railway Wood would become very insecure and every little bit of cover there would be lost.

Hopkins sent me to see Brigadier Butler about the defence of the craters and I got out a scheme for holding the back edges in case the front edges were rushed. There was about a week's work required to dig trenches etc. and the general gave me 150 men for the job. If the Bosch was doing what we thought, it meant working against time – every day the mound of blue sandbags opposite grew higher. We couldn't turn the guns on to it as it was too close to our own line. They were putting up a devil of a lot of wire too, around the mound and the neck of trench up to it, so that there was not much chance of a raid being successful.

It was rather a nasty job digging around the lips of the old craters. They had been blown under our front line sometime in the past and the earth was full of dead, with that nauseating smell of penetrating stale cheese that only month-buried bodies give off.

30th May 1916

On the 30th May, the Shropshires took over that bit of the line and Colonel Wood persuaded the brigadier to let him try a raid on the mound. We had a little conference about it in General[64] Butler's headquarters in the Ramparts and decided that the only way was to get some torpedoes and use them to blow lines in the Bosch wire.

There was a strange man who lived in a little hut in A30 Wood all by himself.

He was a sort of naval lieutenant, dressed in khaki, and seemed to be attached to no unit or division or anything; an independent gentleman, who specialised in torpedoes. He gave demonstrations on demolishing wire entanglements and used to go on raids with the infantry of the 6th Division as a hobby. (Eventually, I believe he disappeared, and was thought to have been captured.)

Hoppy and I went over to see him in the afternoon and were shown the best way of using the things. They were flat tin tubes about 4

All photographs reproduced in this edition are digital copies of the photographs found either in the original script or Bagnold family photograph albums. Photographs are without captions where location of subjects or provenance of photographic image are not known.

The original script, written in 1919.
Bagnold family archives.

Studio portrait of RAB, c. June 1915.
Bagnold family archives.

RAB at Warren Wood, the family home in Kent, June 1915. Bagnold family archives.

RAB and his father (Col. A. H. Bagnold) at Warren Wood, June 1915. Bagnold family archives.

On Leave at Warren Wood, possibly
December 1915.
Bagnold family archives.

Poperinghe c. 1915. Imperial War Museum.

Yser Canal, c. March 1916. Bagnold family archives.

Dawson's Corner, leading to the Yser Canal sector ND. Imperial War Museum.

Street leading from Rue Dixmude in Ypres (now Diksmuidestraat) to the Ramparts, Spring 1916. Imperial War Museum.

Ypres, Spring 1916. Imperial War Museum

The Cloth Hall, Ypres April 1916. Imperial War Museum.

The Cloth Hall, Ypres, c. 1916. Imperial War Museum.

Calais, May or April 1916, L. Verhoustraten (Belgian interpreter), T.A.Smith & RAB. Bagnold family archives.

14. British railway gun, ND. Imperial War Museum.

British heavy artillery, ND. Imperial War Museum.

Bombardment at night, Western Front c.1916. Imperial War Museum.

Arrow-Head Copse, SW of Guillemont, 1st September 1916. Imperial War Museum.

First batch of German prisoners coming in during battle of Guillemont, 3rd September 1916. Imperial War Museum.

Trônes Wood – Guillemont Rd, 4th September 1916. Imperial War Museum.

Ginchy-Flers Road, end of September 1916. Imperial War Museum.

British Mark II or III 'Male' Tank, c. autumn 1916. Imperial War Museum.

Cimetiere des Tanks near Hooge c.1917. Imperial War Museum.

Ypres Ramparts, 1918. Imperial War Museum.

Studio portrait of RAB c.1919.
Bagnold family archives.

inches wide and 5 feet long, fitting one into the other so that you could make any length of torpedo. They were filled with 'Blastine[65]' and you pushed them into the enemy's wire one after the other and loosed them off electrically.

It was quite an exciting little experience that night. We all blacked our faces and hands with burnt cork so as not to show up against the star shells. The Shropshire party crawled out and lay around in the grass while we wormed our way up to the Bosch wire and looked about for a likely place to push the torpedoes in. It was very dark, except when the lights went up. We could see the Bosch sentries every few yards and machine-guns on the parapet through the wire. Very occasionally we pushed in our two torpedoes; the sentry opposite never noticed. Then we crawled back along the electric leads, until we found the shell-hole where we had left the exploder and where the Shropshire officer was waiting. We had a couple of petrol tins full of ammonal too, ready to drop down the supposed mineshaft when we had got into the mound.

Everything was ready when suddenly there was a burst of machine-gun fire from the mound. Lights went up, and they began throwing bombs right among us. We had been spotted, so it was no good going on; besides more than half the party were wounded.

***

The front always got very quiet in the small hours of the night just before daylight. Only in the Canadian sector south of the Menin Road was there any noise. The 3rd Canadian Division was there. They were a new division – wild and irresponsible. From the amount of bombing that went on each night, one would have thought the whole front line garrison got out of their trenches and wandered about no man's land, throwing bombs trees and things in the dark. They seemed bent on annoying the Hun, who all the time maintained an ominous silence.

We walked back down Muddy Lane and along the Menin Road. We usually went back that way in the early morning as it was easier walking than along West Lane trench and things were generally quiet then. West Lane was, of course, safer as you could crouch down in the trench if there was any shelling, but it was long and narrow and winding.

I was always nervous of walking along the Menin Road, especially east of Hellfire Corner. It was so terribly straight and there was nowhere to hide if the Bosch started shooting straight down from Hooge. At Hellfire Corner itself, everybody instinctively walked faster. Any moment a salvo of shrapnel might come shrieking down and burst accurately over the railway crossing.

Every spot on the Menin Road had its name and its traditions of fear. The Culvert, Birr Crossroads, Hellfire Corner, White Château, the last one of the enemy's favourite targets for shelling. Then came our RE dump and the dressing station in the tumbledown houses at the bend in the road. The huge silent *école* in the trees on the left and then the straight bit of road to Suicide Corner. There were the remains of wonderful gardens along that bit of road, all now overgrown with weeds and long grass, and exuding the queer, half-pleasant smell like rank vegetation, and of lachrymatory gas from some tear shells that had fallen there. Lastly there was the open stretch of road from Suicide Corner down past the old cemetery and the big shell hole with the stinking dead mule in it, over the causeway across the moat and in through the Menin Gate. One always hurried to get in under cover of the Ramparts: there was always the feeling that one would be caught on the causeway by a salvo of shells bursting on the Menin Gate.

There was something very wonderful about Ypres, especially in the early morning just before dawn as one came in from the Menin Gate and saw the tall, jagged pinnacles of white stone across the deserted square – the remains of the cathedral and Cloth Hall – with the setting moon in the west shining through. Everything was so hushed and still and there was the feeling of quiet and relaxation on coming home after a long night's work. There was something extraordinary in the acoustic properties of the place. The isolated double bangs of the field guns firing from the ruins and the desultory '*tock tock tock*' of the machine guns a couple of miles away seemed only to enhance the silence in between. The infantry parties in single file skirting the edge of the square seemed to make no noise. You could hear every sound along the front, but sounds originating in the town were somehow damped out.

***

2nd June 1916

On 2nd June, the ominous quiet of the last fortnight was broken. I had gone down to Poperinghe on the company motorbike to buy some things and was on my way back when the bombardment opened. They were shelling the main road behind Ypres pretty heavily, but I found that on a motorbike it didn't worry one much. You couldn't hear the shell coming and you were so intent on dodging the holes in the broken *pavé* to avoid breaking the frame of the bike that there wasn't time to be frightened. Just as I was getting off outside our billet in Rue Dixmude, a shell burst in the air in the street and a splinter took half the carrier away.

The other three – Hopkins, Jackson and Smith – were all there in the cellar when I arrived. Nobody knew what was happening but Hobart, the Brigade Major, had just telephoned through from Brigade HQ in the Ramparts that we were all to stand by.

Every minute the bombardment was getting worse. Soon everything was obscured by brick dust and shell smoke. You couldn't see the cathedral, only 50 yards off across the gardens. Shells were swishing over the broken roof of our house and bursting with great 'Crrrumps' among the ruins.

I had never realised how many of our field guns there were hidden away behind the houses. There seemed to be at least three batteries just behind us within a hundred yards. They were replying for all they were worth just over our heads with that ear-splitting 'pop' that a field gun makes when it is firing almost at one.

Then the tear shells began to arrive and we retired into the cellar and blocked up the entrance. No more sightseeing.

Later in the afternoon, another telephone message came from the brigade. The main Bosch attack was apparently directed on the Canadian front on our immediate right. The General wanted one of us to go over to the Ramparts. I made a dash for it during the first little lull. Down at the end of the street there were ammunition wagons crossing the square at full gallop. I could just see them through the smoke and dust. They were going up to the batteries in front of the moat and along the Menin Road by the *école*.

I dodged round by a backstreet and just got to the Ramparts as a house fell right across the road behind me.

General Butler was sitting smoking in his little office in the cellars under the Ramparts opposite St Jacques Church. He was wearing the old fleece lining of his waterproof that he always wore instead of a tunic. He was just as quiet and self-possessed as when I first met him after dinner in his mess at Calais.

Hobart was reading a telegram from division: 'Following from 3rd Canadians [3rd Canadian Division]' it ran. 'Enemy reported advancing through gap between Hooge and Sanctuary Wood. Situation at Hooge uncertain, believed lost. Our casualties heavy.' The telephone lines forward to our two battalion headquarters at Potijze and the railway bank were both cut and the situation on our front was very uncertain.

The last report had mentioned two mines blown under our front line at A1 and H15, after that nothing.

Then came another message from the Canadians, asking for reinforcements as they had none available within five hours:

> Who've we got, Hobart? Tell the KRRs to send two companies over. Tell them to avoid the railway cutting behind Hellfire Corner, it's full up with gas. Division is sending two companies of the DLI too.

Just then Brace looked in. He'd got a line through to the right battalion. Colonel Wood was on the phone. It appeared the Bosch had attacked on his front too but had been driven off. He had been seen advancing through the gap in the line where the Bellewaardebeek [stream] flowed through, between H15 and Hooge, but apparently the machine-gunners in Outpost Farm had done good work and stopped the attack.

By evening things had quietened down. The Canadians must have got some reinforcements up from somewhere and managed to hold the Bosch up for the time.

Next day, the Bosch attacked again along the Canadian front with a terrific bombardment all along the line and on all the roads. I had to go back to see White at Vlamertinghe about some stores. All along the main road there were the remains of gunner horses and ammunition wagons blown to pieces. By the asylum alone, there were seven six-horse teams lying in the road with pieces of horses and harness up in the trees.

By this time things were serious and the people at the back who lived in big châteaux were apparently beginning to sit up and do things. For the first time in fourteen months, the two old, battered trains with improvised armoured locomotives that used to creep up backwards after dark as far as the asylum with working parties and reliefs, were steaming up in broad daylight and unloading reinforcements for the Canadians amid a hail of shrapnel and high explosive. (That was one of the quiet, ostentatious jobs that never received proper recognition. There was an officer, McCreary I think his name was, who ran those trains up from Poperinghe to the asylum every night for years, and in the daytime used to come up with a gang of platelayers and repair the shell holes in the line.)

In the evening, I went up with the section to lay out and dig a new fire-trench parallel to Muddy Lane, so as to form a defensive flank, for at present our right was absolutely in the air. Hooge had been lost and the whole of Sanctuary Wood, and the Bosch had advanced down the Menin Road beyond Birr Crossroads. Gee and Taylor and the jolly old crowd of Durhams were there to help and we got on pretty well in spite of the heavy shelling. Here and there we came across a stump of a tree to show that the place had once been Y Wood. Gee had some yarn about having been in the brigade office when a wire came in from the 14th Corps saying that, it was most important that Y Wood should be 'cleared of the enemy'. We wondered if any member of the 14th Corps staff had ever been anywhere near. 'Cleared of the enemy' indeed; there wasn't cover for a dog to hide.

It felt very queer out there in what was now no man's land, as if we were completely surrounded. The Verey lights along the front, which were the only means one had of locating oneself in the dark, seems to be going up all round. One could see the long, wavy line of lights, stretching back on both sides, to Mount Kemel in the south-west and to Het Sas and Boesinghe in the north-west – only 90° in between.

To the west, in the direction of Ypres, the trees and ruins were flickering in to view with every flash of our guns. The gunners were keeping the lost ground at Hooge under continuous harassing fire. Every now and then there was a huge green flash that lit up the country and the cloud banks above, followed by a crash, a long drawn out, rumbling like thunder and finally a thud that shook the whole ground. The Army Reserve Artillery had been brought up – the great guns that lived in the back areas and came up for any serious battle on any part of the [British] Army front.

The Bosch attacked again during the night. Every man seemed to have a Verey light pistol. You could see them advancing across the valley, a thick line of white and coloured lights.

For the next few nights, things were quieter and we got on with the new flanking trench facing Sanctuary Wood, but on the 6th [June] the bombardment started again all round the Salient, and Observatory Ridge and Hill 62 were lost; but that was the end. We saw in the English papers headlines about 'The Third Battle of Ypres' etc. But the Bosch apparently thought better of it and didn't launch his main attack. He was probably getting nervous about the ominous signs in the south. The Canadians had lost 10,000 since 2nd June, though, and had to be reinforced by the 3rd Division and half the Guards Division.

***

After that, all fear of a Bosch attack on a big scale passed away, and trench raids and other little offensive operations came into vogue. We began to be infused with the idea of the offensive as opposed to the defensive. The staff issued pamphlets on the 'Offensive Spirit' in which were to be found the famous words about the Subaltern asking himself, 'Am I offensive enough?' which caused considerable amusement.

The preparation of emplacements for gas cylinders in the front line took up quite a lot of our time. This was quite a big undertaking. It meant deepening the old front line trench by about 4 feet, digging through layer after layer of old trench-boards, bully beef tins and corpses. The excavations had them to be lined with wooden cases about 20 feet long and a foot wide so as to hold twenty-five cylinders standing upright.

There was to have been a raid on the 12th with the object of destroying any Bosch mineshafts. Jackson and a party from his section were going over with them, but a patrol found the Bosch wire not properly cut by the artillery, so we contented ourselves with simply letting off the gas.

From then on things settled down. We went on with odd jobs, such as building concrete machine-gun emplacements, repairing communication trenches, especially Muddy Lane, and work on cellars etc. in Ypres.

***

1st July 1916

On the 1st July 1916, came the long expected news that the great offensive on the Somme had opened – the last final battle that would end the war! Two days later we saw in the English [news]papers reports of 'Brilliantly successful advance on a twenty-five-mile front ... Our irresistible troops push forward everywhere ... Our casualties very light ...' etc. All the drivelling hypocritical nonsense of Beach Thomas and the others.

For the next fortnight things were comparatively quiet. Raids and gas discharges became more and more frequent. Jackson went over with one raid and did good work, shooting two or three Bosch and capturing two more.

I came to see a lot of Dalgas while we were working on gas emplacements in Railway Wood. Once he showed me his maps and plans of operations. It was when there was another mine scare on; the sound of digging was being reported by the infantry about every hour and anxious platoon commanders would pop down to his dugout and ask his advice. He would always laugh at them and tell them not to be alarmed. Everything was quite alright.

When we were alone he put his finger on the diagram and showed me where a Bosch sap actually was: under our lines at Railway Wood! He was deliberately letting them dig on. They had passed within a few feet of his outermost listening gallery and the listener out at the end, sitting reading endless magazines to keep his mind occupied, reported that they were all still digging hard. They were nearing another listening post further in and were beginning to be heard there too. As long as they could be heard digging things were alright. It was when the digging stopped that it would be time to act. There was a charge all ready at the end of the furthest listening gallery.

Some days afterwards I asked him how his old Bosch were getting on. He had waited until he was sure that there were a nice lot of Bosch up at the face of the sap, and that morning he had blown his charge behind them, cutting them off. There they were, at that very moment, buried alive. And there they'd remain.

***

I always look back on those two months in Ypres as the happiest time in the whole War. We were such a perfect little community – Hopkins, Jackson, Smith and myself. We all lived together in the same cellar under No. 37 Rue Dixmude.

That cellar and its surroundings, its faint smell of damp masonry, and all its noises, through the night, the regular crashes of the field guns across the gardens and by day the 'swish' of Bosch shells over our roof searching for them, I shall never forget. Nor the hot lazy summer afternoons, from the time we got up to dusk when we started work; when we used to sit in the sun in the stone-flagged courtyard reading or writing letters home while one of us played the gramophone on the white painted garden table. Hopkins would light his old pipe and expand as he'd never done before.

Later in the afternoon, when the big shells began to come over and burst with an echoing rumble in the cathedral, we'd sit and watch the clouds of pink dust sprouting up, dimly picturing what the place was like before it collapsed and trapped the British battalion, whose bodies still lay underneath the fallen pillars and stones; until the splinters came rattling down on the stones of the little yard, and Hopkins would get up and go down to the cellar with a sniff as much to say 'Children, you mustn't stay here anymore. Come in out of the rain.'

I never knew such a change come over a man. He got a passion for my gramophone and presently a box of the very best records arrived – real expensive ones – and in the middle of the night, if he thought he was alone in the cellar, he'd creep out of his little niche in the corner, light his pipe, quietly play over a tune to himself and go back to bed.

***

Sometimes in the afternoons we'd go exploring in the unburnt portions of the town where parts of some of the houses still stood and there were interesting things lying about amongst the rubbish in the rooms; pathetically intimate personal things – books of family photos – all the little worthless treasures that no one else sees in a house that one keeps hidden away at the backs of cupboards. It was hard to believe that only two years ago families had lived here and children ran up and down the stairs.

In the middle of each block of houses there were extraordinary little gardens with rare plants, rockeries and fountains. Everywhere there were roses growing luxuriantly. They seem to thrive on the brick dust in the air; huge, wonderful roses that one seldom sees in England except flower shows. And yet nothing was normal and intact. In the middle of a lovely bank of flowers there would be a shell hole with green slime growing on the surface of the water in it, or a heap of freshly fallen bricks near which one became aware of that hot feeling of the face and eyes, and the peculiar smell of tear gas. Outside in the road you would come across little pools of fresh blood on the *pavé* that testified to the regular toll of twenty or thirty killed and wounded every day in the streets of Ypres.

The chief object of those expeditions was the search for still undiscovered wine cellars. Though nearly all the good things in the town have been exhausted after a year of unrestricted scrounging by British troops, there yet remained a certain number of cellars the entrances to which had been blocked up with fallen masonry either during the first great bombardment before the civilians had left, or very soon afterwards. In our spare time we used to go round with a heavy crowbar, thumping the doors of likely houses hoping to find cellars. In this way the cellars of the *Hôtel de Chantellenie* were discovered and although all the thousands of bottles of the best wines were spoilt by the heat of the fire when the place was gutted during the Second Battle [of Ypres], we got large quantities of the hotel crockery with the Ypres coat of arms on it, which were the envy of all who came to mess with us.

On very quiet days we ventured into the body of the cathedral to look for souvenirs. The interior was just a heap of broken carved stone mingled with scraps of a curious glassy looking stuff – the remains of the slate and leaf roof fused together during the fire when the place was burnt.

I think there were more casualties in the cathedral than in any other spot in Ypres. We lost good NCOs and men on several occasions through rescuing wounded Canadians and other souvenir hunters from among the broken pillars and arches.

One afternoon as we were sitting looking across at the Big Tower – one corner and half two adjacent sides of which still rose straight up to the original height of 200 feet, balanced like a pencil stood on end – we remembered that that corner was said to have a staircase in it. I forget who first proposed it, but we ended by going over and climbing in through the little loop-hole window on top of a heap of stone. The spiral stone stairs were all loose, but like children in an old, ruined castle we had to go up.

Every stone in the tower was loose, just resting one on top of the other, and by the amount of dust and broken stone on the steps no one had been up for months and months. The further we went up the more frightened we became. We kept hearing the whine of shells coming. A lucky shot at the base would be almost certain to bring the whole tottering thing crashing down, but there it had stood all these months, a ranging point for the Bosch who used it to register on for the shelling of the square, useless as an observation post for our gunners as it was too dangerous and yet sacred as one of the great features and traditions of the town.

What a wonderful view there was from the top. We could see almost the whole of Flanders. We were higher than any point of the ridge in front and could see miles and miles behind the Bosch lines. The whole front lay spread out below. There were shells bursting round Zillbecke Lake and at Hellfire Corner. It had apparently been used before as an observation post and there were the remains of telephone wires running up the stairs. How the wretched gunner observer must have scampered down like a frightened rabbit when the shell came that took half the outside wall of the staircase away beneath him and cut his telephone wire.

When I look back on that life with the field company up to the time I left them after the dark, hopeless days when the Somme battle fizzled out in the drenching rain and appalling mud of the autumn and winter, the one outstanding impression is the marvellous comradeship and harmony in which we all lived; a state of existence only possible in the presence of some constant physical fear that hung over all of us. It was the return of the primitive fundamental cause that evolved the first human community, the common fear of death from some outside agency over which there was no control.

We did the same work, shared the same dangers and knew the same friends. We were never tired of one another's company. People's characters and individuality lay open like a book and we liked and were amused by every little peculiarity in them. The company mess was the family circle and the division the largest community in which we took any collective interest. It contained all our friends, who shared our experiences and feared the same fears as we did and were about us wherever we went. In the division was centred all our *esprit de corps* and all our pride, and in the fate of the division were wrapped up all our fates.

Directly I found myself among people who lived in the peace and security of Corps Headquarters, I realised with a shock what I had left behind. I seemed to have got out of one world into another in which something was missing. The people were no longer natural; they no longer said what they thought, and there were all the artificialities, the little dislikes and the feeling of irritation with one's fellows, the unnecessary small talk and gossip just as they exist among any set of people who are forced to see a lot of one another under secure peace conditions.

Chapter 5

THE JOURNEY SOUTH – HÉBUTERNE (JULY–AUGUST 1916)

16th July 1916

We were relieved on the 16th July by the 2nd London Field Company of the 6th Division to whom we handed over our cellars and dugouts in Ypres and moved back to the rear billet at Vlamertinghe.

Next day, the dismounted men were taken back to Houtkerque by the little metre-gauge tramway, running from the cheese market in Poperinghe. We managed to get an excellent billet at Houtkerque in one big farm outside the village. The people were charming, and we could get cream from them and altogether we thought we were in for a good time.

On the following morning, Hopkins came into the mess with a puzzled expression and a telegram in his hand. 'I can't understand it', he said. 'We must be starting an offensive tomorrow, and yet we can't be. We've got orders to march to somewhere behind the Bosch lines near St. Éloi.' It was as well to be prepared for emergencies, so we dumped all our spare kit and a good deal of our mess gear including all our Ypres crockery with the people of the farm who promised to look after it. Gone were all our visions of a nice comfortable rest.

Just as we were on the point of starting, Hobart (the Brigade Major) happened to ride past and we found out that he had given us the wrong map reference and that our destination was really Berthen, in quite a different direction and not as exciting as we thought. It was a hot and dusty march. We went through Abeele and Boeschepe and up over the hills by Mont Kokreele.

19th July 1916

Next morning, we were off again and marched through Bailleul and on to Neuve Eglise where we bivouacked for the night. All along the road from Bailleul onwards there were signs of great activity: broad gauge railway lines running along the sides of the road on both sides; sidings half-finished and parks of lorries everywhere. Near Neuve Eglise, the camouflage people had been busy. There were screens on the side of the road facing the Bosch and on the Bosch side of these the real road was painted so that transport could pass behind while from the front it appeared as an open empty road with never a sign of life. At intervals, sidings ran off from the railway along the road, sidings covered up with imitation grass and ending in imitation houses meant to conceal big railway guns.

We were apparently to take over from the 24th Division and a bit of the 50th (Northumbrian) Division; more particularly we ourselves had orders to take over the front line work from the 103rd Field Company and in the afternoon most of us went round the line with the offices of the other company.

It was the sector immediately east of Mount Kemmel and the front line lay in the hollow between the slopes of Kemmel and the Wytschaete – Messines Ridge, which the Germans held. It was wonderfully quiet, more like Laventie, except for the hilly nature of the country. The great feature of the place was Mount Kemmel. It is the easternmost of the curious range of sugar-loaf hills (Cassel Mont-des-Cats, Mont Kokereele, Mont Noire, Mont Vidaigne, Mont Rouge, Scherpenberg and Kemmel) that run due east to west and rise abruptly out of the flatness of the rest of the country. It is about 500 feet high, was covered with a dense growth of trees, and dominated the whole country around.

Everywhere here too there were signs of abandoned preparations for an offensive. We were shown the entrance to the celebrated Spanbrouckmolen mine, which had been dug right under the German lines on the Wytschaete – Messines Ridge and was loaded with forty tons of ammonal.

Why the great attack on the Messines Ridge was abandoned for a year I never learnt. It was believed to have been due to the explosion of the gigantic ammunition dump at Audruicq between St Omer and Calais, in which all the reserve ammunition for the First and Second Armies destroyed itself in three days and nights of continuous detonation.

There was some muddle over the handing over when we got back. The moving of so many divisions was apparently too much for the high-brows on the staff. Here were three divisions, the 20th, 24th and

50th all quarrelling over the same little sector of the line. They all had orders to leave and each was trying to hand over to the others. Here is an extract from Hopkins' war diary:

> 21st July. Marched to Dranoutre, took over billets and workshops of 103rd Field Coy [Company] and 24th Div[ision], RE dumps there and at Locre, with about 100 Durhams. Workshops officer visited shops of 104, 103 and 129 Field Coys [Companies]. Major Hopkins took note of all work from OCs 103 and 104 Field Coys and saw OC Northumbrian Field Coy about works which had already been handed over to him by 103 and 104 Coys.
>
> 22nd July. Marched to St Jans Cappel at 10[.00] am. Orders to march received at 9.15 am and to hand over works and billets to 7th Field Coy. Spoke to OC 7th Field Coy on the telephone and left 2nd Lieut.[66] Jackson to hand over OC 7th Field Coy refused to take over as he said he had no orders to do so. 2nd Lieut. Jackson reported to the CRE 20th Div.[67] in the afternoon and received instructions to withdraw his party if no officer arrived to take over before the company marched.

23rd July 1916

That night (23rd July) we bivouacked in a field near St Jans Cappel. It rained a bit during the night but most of the company managed to find some shelter under the transport. The officers congregated under one of the GS wagons, except Hopkins who had the underneath of the 'country' wagon to himself.

***

Early next morning, we were on the march again and fetched up at Hondeghem in the afternoon. By this time, we had given up all attempts to find any organised idea or scheme in all this moving about, popping in and out of the line, taking over units and having to hand over again in a few hours. It was just 'Our Brilliant High-Command', playing a game of trying to move troops about like chessmen, like a beginner who moves a piece without thinking ahead and then has to waste other moves trying to correct his bad start. No. It was so far beyond us that it wasn't any good worrying what the staff was up to.

24th July 1916

That evening we really did get some definite orders. We were to march to Bavinchove and entrain for Doullens right down in the Fifth Army area.

It was quite a relief when the train actually started at 21.30 [hours] on the following evening. We were half expecting some counter orders right up until the last moment. We were all very glad to get away from Flanders. We wanted a change. Besides there was the excitement going towards the Somme. Not that we were entirely without presentiments of what was going to happen to us there, but the feeling was very strong. I thought that this was the great battle of the war, and that we ought on no account to miss it. We were proud of the division and wanted it to have a chance of showing itself in battle.

We got to Doullens at about 5.00 am next morning feeling very frowsy and sleepy. We de-trained as quickly as we could and marched off up the little narrow valley to Lucheux about 5 miles north-east, where we found some wretched little billets allotted to us which were in a filthy condition of dirt.

***

What a difference there was in the country here from what we had hitherto seen of France. In the valleys it looked quite like England, with their thickly wooded sides and little fishy streams at the bottom. We missed the scattered, isolated farms of the north and the solid, well-to-do towns like Cassel and Hazebrouck. The villages we passed seemed so squalid and flimsy – just mud and thatch. Where in Flanders a company could be billeted in a single farm, here a whole village was required. Lucheux itself seemed a little better than the other places we passed on the way. It is a pretty little place with a wonderful old castle.

We weren't to stay there long, however. That same afternoon we started off again along the same road we had come up in the morning, and on to Sarton where we joined the rest of the 60th Brigade and bivouacked for the night.

27th July 1916

The next day (27th July) we marched on to Vauchelles and the brigade bivouacked again. Hopkins, Jackson and I went on to Courcelles to see the 151st Field Company of the 38th Division and to take over from them, leaving White, Holgate and Smith to bring the company on next morning.

Courcelles was a miserable place. There were only one or two brick houses, the rest were all mud. The house in which the 151st [Field] Company left was about the only habitable one in the village. The place had not been shelled, merely occupied by troops. All the civilians were gone, the thin mud walls of the houses had fallen down leaving the roofs intact standing on a slender skeleton of wooden posts and laths.

The heat was terrific and the heavy atmosphere of dust and flies, strengthened the general impression of dilapidation.

We went round the line in the morning and Hopkins decided that Courcelles was too far back for us to live and at the same time at work up forward, so Jackson, Smith and I with our sections went to live at Collincamp in some empty dugouts we found in an orchard where a 9.2-inch howitzer battery had lived recently.

Collincamp was even more tumbledown than Courcelles; there were signs that it had been shelled as well as gutted by years of occupation by French troops. The whole country seemed to have been poverty-stricken before the war. The soil was very unfertile and had evidently been merely used for grazing. The land was quite open except where the little woods and tree-surrounded villages were dotted about. There were no isolated farms as in the north. The sparse population had lived only in the miserable clusters of hovels that represented villages, between which lay open chalky land and hedgeless roads.

The whole of this part of Picardy consists of a more-or-less flat plateau, intersected with little deep valleys, wooded in the northern part and getting bearer and bearer towards the Somme and the Santerre country in the south.

***

The bit of the line which our brigade was to hold lay between Hébuterne and Serre. This part of the front had been taken over from the French in the spring of the year and had been at the northern extremity of the great initial attack on the 1st July, which had extended from Gommecourt in the north to Estrées on the Amiens–St Quentin road in the south. Prior to the attack, the line must have been the quietest imaginable. There can have been no fighting or even shelling of any sort. The beautiful deep trenches which the French had dug in the firm sandy soil just above the chalk or in the chalk itself were lined with flowers and grasses that had never been disturbed.

The whole of the offensive down to Thiepval had been a complete and ghastly failure. Hardly a yard of advance had been made anywhere. Now, nearly a month afterwards, all the guns had been taken away and sent down to the southern part of the line, and the Hébuterne sector ceased to be a battle front, relapsing into something like its former calm, at least as far as guns were concerned.

Our front line ran roughly 50 yards to the east of the line of the four copses named 'Matthew, Mark, Luke and John', which were really little old chalk quarries cut into the side of a little valley that ran just behind them. The Bosch line ran along parallel but further up the rise so that on going down into the hollow to get towards the front line you came under observation from the Bosch on the other side. At the bottom, however, and on the east side near the copses you were under cover from view.

It was in the four copses, in the front line and in the assembly trenches below that the ill-fated brigades of the 31st Division assembled for the 'Great Push' of 1st July. They were still there a month later! The Bosch, who knew the exact hour and minute of the attack, probably from listening sets, concentrated all his artillery accurately on them in the trenches and buried them. There they lay by the hundred, by the thousand, under the sandy soil which, loosened by the rain and the bombardment, collapsed filling up what remained of the shattered trenches. A few companies only managed to advance and reached the outskirts of Serre before they were either wiped out or captured.

> I may, perhaps, claim to be in a position to estimate methods and results. I watched the night bombardments, both British and German. I saw at close quarters the hurricane of the morning bombardment, which heralded that first gay, impetuous and irresistible leap from the trenches…!!
>
> Before the day was far advanced, I had discussed their experiences with the plucky, merry groups of our more lightly wounded, who were hurried back like parties of beanfeasters – so gay they held themselves – in processions of brakes and lorries. Some of them did the journey from the third German line to one of our excellent casualty clearing stations within an hour or two!![68]
>
> Beach Thomas[69] in *The Daily Mail,*
> 1st July 1916

All along the Front from Gommecourt to La Boiselle the same sort of thing had happened, and our losses had been so great that all chance of an immediate breakthrough were gone. Gough's Fifth Army, the famous 'Army of Pursuit' which was in readiness behind the Fourth Army had to come up to take over half the Fourth Army's front, so that all the immediately available divisions were used up.

***

Our principal work, as had been that of the 29th Division before us, was the clearing up of the line so as to make it both defensible and habitable again.

The certainty and accuracy of the Bosch information as to the British plans for the attack in this sector were shown by his confining his artillery fire entirely to the assembly trenches in the little valley and to the front line. Three hundred yards or less behind the front line nothing had been touched. It remained the old peaceful trench area just as the French had left it. There were all the refinements and comforts of 'peace warfare' that the French was so fond of. There was a complete water supply with a pumping station in La Signy Farm; there were distribution pipes and water tanks in the trenches at each battalion headquarters; beautiful deep trenches laid out regularly like a chessboard with communication trenches and cross trenches, all named and covered with noticeboards and arrows.

Forward of Battalion HQ and down the slope into the hollow, the contrast was extraordinary. You saw merely a mass of brown earth and white chalk, simmering in the heat. As you went on, the trench almost disappeared; the dry, dusty earth was spongy to walk on; every yard or two there were damp patches, half-hidden under a swarm of big green-backed flies. Sometimes you'd pass a procession of stretchers heralded by an overpowering smell of rotten cheese and a cloud of flies – a new bit of the of front line was being opened up, and they were removing the old occupants to dumps further back for burial – heaps of rags and rotten flesh over which the flies droned and hissed in the stifling heat.

***

The work of the company was concentrated entirely on the construction of tunnel dugouts and deep trench mortar emplacements, except for Smith's section, which looked after the water supply and tramways.

Jackson and I each had two big trench mortar emplacements, and two tunnel dugouts in the front line to hand. It was nice straightforward work. We had three reliefs of men, mostly gunners, for each emplacement and infantry parties for the front line dugouts, so that work was going on all through the twenty-four hours.

All the work consisted of mining, that is driving tunnels downwards into the ground for 20 or 30 feet, fitting in solid frames of 3-inch timber (about 2 feet 6 [inches] wide and 5 feet 6 [inches] high) to support the roof and sides of the tunnel, and afterwards excavating the actual dugout chamber at the bottom. The trench mortars had dugouts and in addition the actual emplacement, which consisted of a square pit like an inverted pyramid about 20 feet square at the top and tapering down to a few feet at the bottom, twenty feet below. They were for the new 10-inch trench mortar that fired a 150-pounder bomb.

At that time, we had no trench mortars in the area at all with which to reply to the Bosch who, having taken all his guns away to the battle front as we had done, had armed himself with dozens of the horrid things.

A heavy trench mortar bombardment, especially at night, is one of the most terrifying things, far worse than shells, machine guns, or aeroplane bombs. They are so slow. They seem to take an infinity of time hovering in the air above – a train of sparks going up, up, up from the enemy's lines, and then, if it is going to fall close to you, seeming to remain stationary forever over your head while you cower down at the bottom of a shell hole or trench with your mind a blank, waiting. Then the faint fluttering rush, no louder than that of a golf ball in flight, as it comes down almost vertically, then bursting with a terrific detonation like no shell in the world. There is no shelter from it. You feel as unprotected in a trench as in the open.

Some nights, trench mortar bombs used to come over in showers, bursting either in the front line or in the hollow behind. Several times they put our infantry carrying parties to flight, leaving most of their load of mine frames, sandbags, etc. all along the trench.

By day, there was a dead silence in the forward area save for an occasional thud as a Bosch rifle grenade burst on one of our communication trenches, and an almost imperceptible murmur from the myriad green corpse-flies as they swarmed about the damp dark patches in the dry earth. The sun blazed down into the little breathless valley and made the brown surface of the ground hover in the heat as you looked at it, and the whole air was permeated with the stink of decaying men.

For the first few days after we arrived we were still suspicious that we might easily be ordered to move away again just as we had got to know the new front and organised our work. The ways of the staff are incomprehensible.

However, at the end of the week we settled down to things. The prevailing idea was that we were only here temporarily, for a few weeks perhaps before moving down to the Fourth Army on the Somme.

There were a lot of speculations as to whether we should continue to belong to the 14th Corps and whether the other divisions, the Guards and the 6th were following us down from Ypres. The division was very proud of itself belonging to the 14th Corps, the Corps d'Elite. We came to the conclusion that we would probably come in for the climax of the battle, and there was talk of the 14th Corps being the 'Corps of Pursuit'. The great battle was still going on and everyone was very optimistic. It was still going to be the final battle of the war. At nights you could watch the Verey lights and flashes of the guns to the south and hear the distant rumbling bombardments. The 38th Welsh Division whom we had relieved was still somewhere about and they were odd units of it at Collincamp with us. They had been at Mametz Wood[70] and from all accounts had fared badly owing to rotten staff work and were going to some quiet bit of the line to recoup. We heard all kinds of stories from them of the battle – fabulous tales of the number of guns and heavy howitzers we had.

10th August 1916

On the 10th August, Hopkins left the company to become CRE of the 39th Division. It came as a great shock. We none of us realised how much we owed to him until he was gone, or the affection we had for him. It didn't seem to be the same company for a long time afterwards. I missed him particularly because I had been with him so much longer than the others. He was the one connecting link with the dear old days at Laventie that now seemed infinitely long ago. I began to feel a kind of patriarch.

Pennycuick, the new OC was a regular officer with only about four years' service. He had been out at the beginning of the war and got a DSO[71] and been wounded.

A new French interpreter arrived about the same time. His name was Chiney or something like that. He was a silent, seemingly morose sort of man, and as Pennycuick, following a distrust of interpreters that he had learnt at the beginning of the war wouldn't have him in our mess, we saw very little of him.

***

15th August 1916

On the 15th August, we were relieved by our old friends of the 75th Field Company of the Guards Division. We marched off the following morning, picking up the mounted section of the company at Cogneux and going on through St Leger, Authie, Thievers to Amplier where we went into billets for the night. At 5.00 am we were on the march again and went through Doullens, Candas, Fienvillers and down a long steep hill into a tiny village called St Hilaire.

We used to enjoy that marching. It was no effort now. There is always a great feeling of pleasure in marching in a long column of men and transport. It's the swing of it and the sound of it, and most of all the idea of collectiveness that grows out of the steady tramp of men and the waves of song that surge forwards and backwards along the columns.

17th August 1916

Next morning, all the transport and cyclists marched off under White and Jackson towards the south, while the rest of us remained at St Hilaire for the day.

We were being introduced to the 'Tactical Train', a staff experiment in moving troops. The great point in the system seemed to be that it caused the greatest complication in orders and in the distribution of rations, and it split the whole division up into mounted and dismounted portions so that it was rendered useless for any emergency for two days.

Next day, having received no orders, Pennycuick took us off back to Candas which we had passed on the last march. We arrived just in time to find our train with half the 60th Brigade in it in the act of starting. Scott, too, appeared with the 84th Field Company a few minutes afterwards but there wasn't any room for them. He apparently hadn't had any orders either.

The only difference between a Tactical Train and any other train, as far as the actual train itself was concerned was that it went slower. We took seven hours to do the journey of about 30 miles, wandering all round by Canaples, Condé-Foile and Amiens and eventually arriving at 7.00 pm at tock on the Ancre.

We marched off at once up the valley to Ville-sur-Ancre and bivouacked among the trees at the edge of the river. White and the transport arrived a little while afterwards and we made ourselves comfortable with what tarpaulins etc. we had accumulated and hidden in the pontoons.

It was nice and cool on the grass under the trees near the river, an ideal camping ground. All along the bank the other units of the brigade were pulling in and settling down for the night, and soon fires began to spring up everywhere as the cooks got to work on the evening meal.

Chapter 6

THE SOMME (AUGUST–SEPTEMBER 1916)

21st August 1916

Next morning, the 21st August, we marched up the valley past the great railway sidings between Dernancourt and Méaulte, full of trains loaded with railway material, waiting to push on as the line advanced. Through the long straggly, dirty mud village of Méaulte and off to the right, up to a camping ground on the slopes of the hills just above the Albert–Bray road: the Sandpits Camp.

The hot weather still continued. Troops and transport were moving in the dust along that white chalky roads like columns of ants.

Three valleys joined just east of Méaulte forming a huge amphitheatre, surrounded by the chalk down of short, parched grass seamed with zig-zagging trenches of bare white chalk. To the north, about a mile away, hidden behind a spur that ran westward from the hills, lay Albert. The famous tower with the huge gilt virgin stretching out horizontally as though in the act of diving, just showed over the ridge. To the east, up the main valley, lay the little village of Bécourdel and beyond that, 2.5 miles away, the hills closed in forming a natural gateway to the rising country further east. Here you could just see a patch of white chalk and dust that was probably Fricourt. Above us there hung a great bank of balloons, stretching away as far as one could see; we counted thirty-seven of them. The wind was in the west and they seemed to be sweeping forward on their ropes – a sort of symbol of the Great Offensive. Between them and round them and over them the aeroplanes were uncountable. They were everywhere in all directions in the sky.

Above the drone of the aeroplanes, there was the steady, indefinable sound of transport, which emanated from everywhere at once and seemed to be part and parcel of the shimmer in the air above the ground. Then came a nearer, louder noise, the tramp of infantry and the jingling of water carts. The 60th Brigade was arriving and settling down in the lower part of the camp.

All of a sudden, towards evening, the earth began to vibrate and the air throbbed and thumped with an all-pervading irregular rumble – the most wonderful stirring sound in the world, the throbbing of a great bombardment. We looked to the east, to the ridge beyond Fricourt. The sun was still shining on it yet over and above the sun's reflected light, the distant slopes of the ridge were scintillating with the green flames of the guns. We watched it, fascinated. We had a feeling of wonder at this inconceivable liberation of energy. We realised, subconsciously perhaps, that this was something greater in intensity of energy than had been achieved by man since the world began.

Two hours later when the bombardment had died down and the darkness was coming on, a comparative silence fell on everything. One by one, lights appeared on the dim slopes of the hills until presently the whole great amphitheatre was lit up with myriad tiny twinkling points of light interspersed here and there with larger, duller yellow glows of camp fires. Again, we became aware of that peculiar rustling murmur, much fainter than before – the murmur of countless thousands of little groups of men sitting talking round their guttering candles before going to sleep.

It was the great camp of the British Army. Never before had any of us realised the immensity of the struggle or the size of the armies involved. Here were the whole national efforts of two great nations, the two greatest nations in the world, directed against one another, all in the space of a few miles.

Each one of those hundreds of thousands camping in the open over the undulating downs must have been thinking the same thing, marvelling, vaguely perhaps, at the number of men which that ocean of little lights represented. And the combined eternal effect of their thoughts probably went to intensify the fascination, the terror almost, which one felt in the presence and the latent power of such a gigantic human congregation organised and existing for one sole purpose. It was a strange feeling and one that could only come to a person under like conditions. Probably it was that feeling of unbounded collective mightiness that drew together the vast armies of Genghis, of Alexander and Napoléon in the past, holding them together when otherwise they would have just melted away.

What a small unit we were in the midst of this little army sleeping in the open. The dying glows of the little campfires and the yellow pinpoints of light spread out in all directions following the folds in the ground; and out of sight in valley after valley to the north and south we could picture them spreading out, on and on.

How small our own division was: a mere 20,000 men. How impotent we all were with regard to our own fate, even the division as a whole. It might be wiped out like the 31st had been at Hébuterne. It was all a matter of luck.

***

22nd August 1916

Next day, the 22nd August, we marched up through Fricourt and along the valley to Carnoy. We had to keep off the roads, which were reserved for lorries and which were quite inadequate even for them. For 50 yards on each side of the roads, the ground was worn bare and smooth with the continuous stream of traffic, troops and waggons going backwards and forwards. Everywhere, too, there were cross-country tracks blocked with horse transport and troops on the march. Luckily the ground was still hard.

We were extremely interested in Fricourt. It was the first time we had captured enemy trenches. During a ten-minute halt we all left the track and saw as much as we could of what was left of the village, the German trenches and their celebrated dugouts. We marvelled at the size of the shell holes and the number of dud 9.2- and 12-inch shells lying about.

There were so many things that were absolutely new to us. The tremendous traffic on the roads; the rows of great long 6-inch guns firing in the open with no attempt at concealment and the water supply arrangements – these were elaborate water troughs to water hundreds of animals at a time, fed by miles of pipelines. Also the balloons whose ropes were fixed to lorries, which drove about the country like boys with kites.

The country itself was so new. The short dry grass on the downs was intersected by brown tracks and snow-white streaks of thrown-up chalk where the trenches ran.

A little further on the left we saw Mametz Wood where the 38th Welsh Division had had the sad experiences of the battle. Then Mametz village: a few fragments of wooden roof on the side of the hill, already overgrown with grass.

Towards Carnoy, the little valley at the bottom of which the road ran was lined with howitzers, battery after battery of 8 inch and 9.2s, all surrounded with heaps of ammunition and lorries unloading still more shells. We had always regarded a 9.2-inch howitzer as something rather wonderful. We had seen them occasionally in ones and twos hidden away in woods and concealed with great care. Here they were strewn about everywhere.

At Carnoy we met one of the field companies of the 24th Division again and took over their living accommodation which consisted of fairly comfortable dugouts in the east side of the valley about 20 feet from the bottom.

There was very little left of the 24th Division now. It was broken for a long time to come. Like the 31st Division north of the Ancre and many, many others they had tried and failed, and now they were going away to some quiet spot to recuperate and absorb reinforcements to fill the empty husks of their battalions.

***

Carnoy itself consisted, as far as the village itself was concerned, of four or five structures bearing some resemblance to houses spread out up the hill leading to Montauban. Our dugouts were just on the right of this road, and on the corner of the valley which here takes a turn to the east.

It was a busy spot. At the bottom of the valley, the French were repairing the metre-gauge railway which used to run from Albert through Guillemont to Combles and Péronne. The rest of the flat part of the valley was taken up with lines of water troughs, surrounded with scores of horses and mules. Just beneath us too, about 50 yards away, was a battery of 9.2-inch howitzers, which prevented us from ever keeping a candle alight for more than a quarter of an hour at a time. How we hated that battery after the first day. When we were outside the dugout we were continually on the lookout, waiting for any indication that a gun was going to fire; then up would go our hands to our ears and we'd wait for the shock. Next door to us was a dressing station and little groups of wounded hung about outside waiting to be attended to. Very often there were shell-shock cases there, but the howitzers had to fire just the same. It was pitiful sometimes.

I think it was that afternoon that our enthusiastic idea of the newfound efficiency, organisation and omniscience of the staff became slightly dimmed. First of all, we thought, here was this railway running along the whole length of the valley, repaired and yet wholly unused save by the little party of French who ambled up each morning pushing a truck or two with sleepers and rails and ambled back to Albert in the evening. There were also along that valley at least a hundred heavy howitzers within 30 yards of the line and yet all their ammunition was brought up by innumerable lorries which could only carry half a dozen shells at a time – brought up for miles in endless crawling convoys along crowded roads. It seemed to us that something was wrong somewhere. Secondly, there was this dressing station, just above four gigantic howitzers. There seemed to be some lack of coordination or liaison. However, the ways of the mysterious staff who lurked in places of fabulous luxury far behind the lines were quite beyond our ken.

***

23rd August 1916

Next morning, the 23rd, Pennycuick took Jackson and me and all the section sergeants up to have a look at things in the line. Up the hill towards Montauban we came on the 60th Brigade bivouacked just off the road near the original front line, on what shortly afterwards became 'The Craters Camp'. Further on, after we had passed the remains of Montauban, the road began to deteriorate rapidly, and a jumble of entangled lorries, motor ambulances and staff cars – many with swearing drivers – trying to turn round marked the end of things as far as motor transport was concerned.

The Bosch was very quiet that morning, although the lazy firing of our guns every half an hour or so must have amounted, on the other side, to quite a bombardment in itself. We turned to the left at Bernafay crossroads and followed a track on the edge of a new and excellent communication trench, Leinster Alley, which ran east through Bernafay Wood. We got down into the trench just before entering Trônes Wood, followed it through the wood and on into the open on the other side, where for the next half mile it got shallower till it averaged only a couple of feet deep.

What a place! Nothing but a wavy sea of light brown earth as far as one could see. No, it wasn't all brown earth. It was speckled with little dark bundles of rags and equipment. The further we went, the thicker they became. The trench was now no more than a series of craters joined together roughly by shallow cuts through the lips from one to the other. In a few places, energetic men had dug it fairly deep for a yard or two till they had to become too sickened to do any more.

It was nothing but one great shambles. Everywhere the ground was full of dead – English dead. They lay in such appalling numbers that we felt like intruders upon them; we were such a few among so many. Those little heaps on the surface of the ground were but a few of them. They were one on top of the other, deep down in the ground. The newly dug trench had exposed portions of men lying in every conceivable position. Here a shoulder projected resting on an elbow; below it two blue-green hands were stretched out into the trench. On the top of the ground, a complete leg severed at the hip, and a few feet further on two faces looked out of the earth: near them the lower half of a man who had been cut in two.

They were fresh. They were only beginning to decay, great green-backed flies were swarming on the ground and rose on our approach like a cloud of smoke. Directly we had passed they settled again, and we could see the winds scintillating under the burning sun.

We were getting near the front line now. A rail lying across the trench gave us an idea of our position. We must be crossing the railway just west of Guillemont Station. And yet there was no sign of the station.

Why weren't we shot at? The trench was only a couple of feet deep and in some places did not exist, and our party was walking in the open with the Bosch only a few hundred yards away; but there was not a sound except the buzzing of the flies. We seemed to be absolutely alone with the army of dead in a strange brown world sweltering in the sun.

***

For six weeks Guillemont, together with Thiepval and Posiers, had held up the advance. The fine weather might be over any day and yet at no place had we been able to set foot on the main ridge. Division after division had been brought up, fresh keen divisions like ours, composed of the very best class of officers and men the British Army ever had in the war, the 'First and Second Hundred Thousand', now fully trained and hardened by a year at the front. And they had failed.

All around lay the remains of the 3rd Division and after them the 24th Division who had failed the first time and had been ordered to attack again and again until there was nothing left of them. Now it was our turn. Would the 20th Division succeed where the others had failed?

We began to think of the infantry in a very different light. Up to now we had thought of them more or less from our own point of view only, that is as people who lived in the front line and supplied working parties for us. Now our estimation of our own position shrank to something like its proper proportion as we realised what they had to look forward to. They had no chance of living on. If they succeeded now, it probably only meant another show afterwards somewhere else; and if they failed the price of failure was written deep into the ground wherever they chose to look. We passed odd platoons of them that morning in the line: they were merely existing, crouching down in chains of hollows in the ground all mixed up with the bodies of the men who had been before them.

23rd August 1916 (continued)

That night, I went up again with the section and a large working party of the Durhams to start work on new assembly trenches. We tramped slowly along Leinster Alley all the way from Bernafay Wood as we were afraid of losing our way in the dark over the open. We got into the middle of Trônes Wood when violent machine gun fire started from the trenches in front, and Verey lights went up in showers. At the same time the Bosch shells began to come over. We could hear their explosions echoing through the wood and the crash of falling trees as more shells fell in the wood itself. The long column of men, jammed in the trench, came to a final standstill. It was no good trying to go on while this lasted so we waited.

I remember being very frightened that night. It wasn't the shells – we were always frightened of them – it was the fear of the unknown. At Laventie, on the canal and even at Ypres we had understood the war. We knew the worst the Bosch used to do in each particular sector. But here it was a new kind of war altogether: colossal and inhuman. There was a continual feeling that at any moment, one's whole section, and with it every landmark in the spot where it was, might be blotted out by this new kind of intensity of artillery fire that made whole villages untraceable. Whole brigades were blotted out in unsuccessful assaults and no one seemed to care. Other brigades, other divisions were sent up to attack again over the mixture of flesh and earth that only a few days before had been clean fields and grass downs. There seemed to be no soul left in the war. We were just little particles of a vast inexorable machine, clumsily and inefficiently controlled by vague, impersonal and unfeeling beings, who didn't, who couldn't know, and who didn't seem to care about the details of the working out of their ultimate schemes. At that very moment, the infantry of our own brigade, many of whom we had known since the Laventie days were probably being killed and wounded out there in front of Guillemont where those shells were bursting incessantly.

24th August 1916

The next night I went up with Pennycuick and a couple of NCOs to lay out the assembly trenches for the next attack on Guillemont. A new scheme had been devised, it having been at the last decided that a frontal attack offered small prospect of success. Our existing front line to the north of the village ran out in a little salient nearly to the Waterlot Farm–Guillemont road. To the north of the right-angled corner, which formed the apex of the salient, the trenches faced east towards Ginchy while to the west they faced the north edge of Guillemont.

From a careful study of aeroplane photographs, it had been found that the Bosch did not appear to have any regular trenches directly opposite the salient. He probably only had a few men lying out in shell holes. Our orders were to push a trench out eastward for a couple of hundred yards, if possible, and then turn north, parallel to the Waterlot Farm road, thus forming a square of trenches, jutting out towards the Bosch. Several lines of trenches at right angles to each other, were then to be dug within the square to form a kind of grid.

Luckily it was a quiet night. Except for one of our 9.2-inch batteries, which insisted on firing short into our own trenches, we weren't bothered with shells much. There were no landmarks of any kind, and it was a very dark night, so we had to do everything by compass bearings and 50-yard lengths of tape. We spent quite a long time hunting for the Waterlot Farm road and only guessed where it had been by the extra number of loose stones lying about.

By the time the two companies of the DLI arrived to do the digging, we had it nearly all marked out for them. The Durhams were absolutely irrepressible on these occasions. They made as much noise getting to work as they did at their billets in the rest areas behind the lines fighting over their breakfasts. We could hear them behind us as we were finishing marking out the foremost trenches, swearing and laughing as they sank into the earth, digging at an incredible speed. We caught three or four Germans during the night at the bottom of shell holes and the noise they made quarrelling over the wretched fellows' helmets and equipment should have aroused all the Bosch in Guillemont. I don't suppose there was much noise really, but when one doesn't know where the enemy are in the dark and finds parties of them in odd shell holes, every sound seems tremendous.

***

28th August 1916

On the 28th we handed over the work on the grid to the 96th Field Company and Story and Formby finished it off with the help of the Durhams. Now we concentrated on other preparations. We had large infantry parties working on the communication trenches, Leinster Alley and Trônes Alley. We also started cutting tracks through Trônes Wood and Bernafay Wood, which were still very dense in spite of the tremendous shelling to which they had been subjected.

Except for the infantry who had originally captured these two woods, and the pioneer battalion of the 24th Division who had dug Leinster Alley right across them, nobody had had occasion to enter them except by the trench, over the edge of which you could see the black trees looming overhead as you passed through.

I never think of Trônes Wood except as some morbid dreadful creation of Edgar Allan Poe. It always seemed to be dark there in spite of the clearances made by the breaking and falling of many of the trees. The thick undergrowth, torn about by the bursting of shells underneath, was tangled in the inextricable confusion with the fallen and dying branches of the trees above. Up among the boughs above there hung long shreds of clothing and here and there pieces of German bodies, while beneath dead Germans sprawled in little clusters round the remains of heavy guns half buried under huge logs which had formed the roofs over the elaborate gun pits, now mere heaps of wreckage.

***

On the 27th, the long spell of dry scorching weather came to an end with a deluge of rain. The trampled footpaths over the scattered earth between the shell holes immediately got a film of greasy mud over them, which made it very hard to keep one's footing. Off these tracks, one's boots collected in a few paces so much of the loose wet mud that they could hardly be lifted.

With the rain and the increasing depth of the mud came a heavier and heavier bombardment by the Bosch and an increasing proportion of gas and tear shells. Night after night we marched up the long interminable road through Montauban to Bernafay Wood in the rain and the 6 inches of slush washed down into the sunken road from the crumbling earth on the sides. Hitherto the shelling had been confined in a surprising manner to Trônes Wood and the ground and trenches in front of it. Now the danger zone was spreading further and further back. Between Montauban and Bernafay Wood particularly the Bosch began to drop heavy stuff either to catch the jumble of traffic floundering in the mud or to worry the batteries on either side of the road. Sometimes you could see them bursting in the road ahead while you were marching steadily nearer and hoping that it would stop before you got there. Sometimes in the darkness a great red glare would rise up silently from somewhere away to the side, lighting up the whole landscape for a few seconds like the glare from an open furnace door, and dying down again only to make the night darker than before. What was it? Something unknown, perhaps some new frightfulness launched by the Bosch, perhaps only a small dump of field gun ammunition set alight.

On the road behind Bernafay Wood we'd pick up our infantry working party. All along that road as far as the bottom of the hollow, was almost one continuous line of dumps of Mills bombs, Stokes mortar bombs and 18-pounder shells all mixed up with our dumps of RE material: barbed wire, timber etc. Sometimes a shell would land in the middle of a dump of bombs and start them off burning and detonating one after the other, like Chinese crackers and scattering the hundreds of troops waiting in the dark for guides or REs. Always there were dead and wounded here, and shouts for stretcher bearers. Always there was the smell of tear gas.

From Bernafay Wood, the rest of the journey lay over the bare earth now turned into mud wherever a regular track was formed. In front was the dark outline of Trônes Wood lying right across the little valley, the black stumps of the trees flashing out intermittently into silhouette against the yellow light of the bursting shells along the front edge, which was always a favourite barrage line for the Bosch. It was a terrifying place, never quiet from the echoing of the guns behind, and the rending crashes of the bursting shells within always heavy with the atmosphere of damp dying timber, decaying bodies and tear gas.

On the last few nights, the gas shelling was very trying. The work had to be done, but when the air got too bad, there was nothing for it but to pull down our gas helmets.[72] It is almost impossible to work on a dark night with the old type of helmet on. You can't see through the eye pieces sufficiently. There always seemed to be gas in the air, now only faint, now too strong to breathe without a helmet.

On 1st September, the last night of work before the battle, there was a drizzling mist. We still had two jobs to finish: dugouts for battalion headquarters and for an aid post. For the first two hours, everything went well except for the rain which made the earth gradually crumble down, bit by bit in soft, sticky lumps. Then, with its own peculiar delicate fluttering noise, the first gas shell came over, bursting with a little sick '*phit*' in the ground 50 yards away. The job had to be finished, so we worked on as long as we could, till the men began to cough and cough and our eyes to stream. Then we had to work in two shifts, one party working for a short spell, while the other was resting and breathing through their helmets. During one bad gust of gas, when we were all waiting at the bottom of a bit of trench with our gas helmets tucked tightly into our coat collars, the earth above began to crumble away and a large thing slithered down to my side and lay there. Presently, I lifted my helmet to see if the air was clear enough to go on working. There was a man lying beside me. Then a Verey light went up and I saw that there was nothing of him existing below the waist except a long, thin rag.

At last things got so bad we couldn't carry on any longer. The job was practically done and we started for home. The tear gas was very thick and hung all along the valley. In Bernafay Wood, it was worse and mixed with another gas that made one want to vomit. At the other side of the wood, it was impossible to keep our helmets off any longer, and we had to grope our way blindly. Through our eyepieces all we could see was an intermittent greenness as the mist was illuminated by the Verey lights at Guillemont. All round there were shouts of men trying to find each other and everywhere there was coughing and curses. The gas shells were raining down. You could hear the whispered flutter of them coming through the air. All along the road we came on the 12th RBs,[73] half the battalion, lying about anyhow. They had just come out of the trenches by Guillemont Quarry after a week in the most appalling conditions any men could exist in. They were absolutely exhausted, and on meeting the gas they'd just sunk down on the road in despair. It was too much trouble to make any effort to get away. They were too exhausted even to want to live on. Why not lie here and get it over? They would have if it hadn't been for four or five indefatigable officers and NCOs. As it was many of them died.

What interminable road it was back to Carnoy! But never mind, there was the thought of hot tea and the rum ration when we got in. I wondered how many of the section would have to go to hospital. I wondered if the pressure on my chest, as if an iron band was round it, would get any worse.

***

We got back just as it was getting late. A few minutes later, I could see a fire going over by the section dugouts and Sergeant Perrin came round for the two whisky bottles full of rum, which was the daily ration for the section. Then I started the primus in the little heart of tarred felt that we used as a mess and got out some bully beef, bread and cheese.

Outside, the thin morning mist was clearing, and I could see the green of the trees along the Péronne road across the valley about 200 yards away and the grass on the slope opposite. Then as the sun rose, first a few, and then columns of horses and mules appeared from all sides for the morning water at the troughs below. The old French sappers came along, pushing their trolley up the little railway with their tools and midday meal on it. Little tails of smoke began to rise from a score of cookhouse fires and the smell of fried bacon filled the air. How quiet and homely it all was.

We had come back into the proper natural world. Already the events of the last fourteen hours were fading out of memory. It was as if we had emerged from a dream existence whose shadow was driven away by the daylight of reality. Only the strange feeling in the chest and a great sleepiness constituted any link with the night.

One lived two lives then, each in an utterly different world. Up in the brown country, where the wasn't even a blade of grass left, at night among the shells and corpses, one's mind seemed to change and become more or less numb to the surroundings – to stand still, always waiting, sometimes consciously, sometimes unconsciously, to be knocked out by a flying splinter. And in the daytime, in the little mess at Carnoy, with all the busy noises of men and horses, and the trundling of lorries along the road, and with the outlook of grass downs and trees, it seemed as if that other country wasn't really there at all; it was merely 4 miles away but distinctly separated by something.

I don't remember much about Carnoy between the time when we got up, about midday, and the time when we started off in the evening. We did nothing particular except hang about in the mess. One meal followed the other with hardly a pause, for there were only five or six hours altogether to eat breakfast, lunch, tea and dinner. There was a dump of RE material on the Maricourt road just across the valley that someone had to look after, and they were in the section dugouts to be inspected and the sections to look after. Sometimes we would stroll down to where they were boring for water at the bottom of the valley and watch the portable boring machine at work. (The whole army was now dependent on the new water arrangements as there were no wells, streams or even ponds in the shelled country. Pipelines were being pushed ahead as fast as possible. They hoped to get a very big supply from Carnoy and were boring half a dozen wells there.)

One picture, I can remember very well: the Prince of Wales,[74] by himself, all splashed with mud, standing in the slush at the bottom of the valley with a bit of stick, poking away at the mudguards of his push bike, clearing out the dirt that had clogged it all up. He was always about with his push bike, in and out of the men's dugouts and wading about the horse lines. Every man in the whole 14th Corps knew him.

3rd September 1916

By 9.15 am on the morning of 3rd September, we had taken up our battle positions in Dummy Trench, about a hundred yards to the west of Trônes Wood and halfway up the north slope of the little valley, and were proceeding to make ourselves as comfortable as we could in the little hollows scratched into the chalk at the bottom of the trench, so as to afford as much cover as possible against the shrapnel and splinters that were bound to come over when the bombardment started. Besides ourselves, Dummy Trench contained Brigade Headquarters at the bottom of a deep dugout (to which a staircase cut in the chalk led down from the side of the trench); one company of the 12th RBs and two companies of Durhams.

Everyone had on his battle kit including a diamond-shaped piece of bright metal about 4 inches long, cut from an old biscuit tin or anything else that came to hand, tied with a piece of string so that it hung down just below the coat collar behind in order to show the observers in the contact patrol aeroplanes above where our troops were and how far they had got. We also had large-scale maps of Guillemont with all the streets named and all the prominent buildings marked, and with the objectives for the day shown. We studied this and practically got to know all the details of the village off by heart.

Each individual settled down to make his own little nest in the chalk at the bottom of the trench. The attack wasn't to start until 11.00 am and we had been told that we probably shouldn't be wanted till a couple of hours after that if all went well.

About half an hour before the bombardment opened, I was sitting on the edge of the trench talking to two of the sappers of my section, Gattrel and Smith, who were digging away at the chalk below, more to pass away the time than anything else, when suddenly there was a thud in the ground beneath my feet that for an instant eclipsed all other sensations, then a violent singing in my ears. The trench was filled with a pungent, acrid smoke. Two khaki heaps were lying one on top of the other at the bottom of the trench, while on the white chalk, little pieces of cloth and red stains were spattered. The thuds continued at intervals of a second or so, accompanied by little violent upwards jerks of the bodies below. A few yards along the trench, Corporal Talbot and another sapper collapsed on the ground, one with blood streaming down his face, and the other holding his stomach with both hands.

Either Gattrel or Smith had put their pick into a buried heap of Mills bombs that were lying under the chalk in the old trench, and they had gone off one after the other till they were finished. The two lads were both quite dead, riddled through and through with splinters. Talbot had an artery out in the arm and ten wounds in the stomach, while the fourth man got off with a flesh wound in the head.

We buried the two dead sappers in a grave dug at the bottom of a large shell hole nearby. There was a padre on the spot, so there was no object in waiting. The two others had to remain where they were for the time as they couldn't be taken back. The whole bomb and ammunition dump behind Bernafay Wood was alight, crackling like enormous holly leaves on a bonfire and completely blocking the road. Every few minutes came a bigger detonation, and a great red flame shot up crowned by an ever spreading mushroom of pink smoke, which floated away into the distance towards Montauban.

Four more of the old hands who had been with the section at Laventie, Bac St Maur, on the canal and at Ypres were gone. There were very few of them left now, only about nine. The rest were quite recent reinforcements.

***

Then the five minutes' intense bombardment just prior to the attack opened up and one forgot everything else in the deafening noise of several dozen field gun batteries firing from behind, just over our heads

In between those piercing barks and the slower hammer blows of the 60 pounders and long-range guns that rolled and throbbed in the air and through the ground, you could hear the soft 'woof, woof, woof' of the great howitzers in the Carnoy valley and the rumbling gurgle of the 9.2-inch shells coming through the air at once. This was to be a final effort to take Guillemont and the 14th Corps' reputation was staked on it. They say there was a gun to every yard and a half of front opposite the village that such a reckless expenditure of life had failed to capture.

Cavan's artillery was now beginning to be talked about, as was his reputation for refusing to allow his troops to undertake the impossible. There was also some talk of a new idea in artillery work, which was now to be tried for the first time – the 'Creeping Barrage'.

The 14th Corps was attacking on the extreme right of the British line and with the French Sixth Army[75] on its right. At that time, it had at its disposal seven divisions, or more than the whole of the original

Expeditionary Force. Of these, three divisions – the Guards, the 56th and the 6th – were in reserve while the remaining four were actually taking part in the attack. On the right, the 5th Division was attacking Falfmont Farm in conjunction with the French. On its left came our division opposite Guillemont and the 16th (Irish) Division cooperating with it on the attack on Guillemont Station. To the left again was the 7th Division opposite Ginchy.

It was a general attack on the whole battle front by the British Fourth Army and the French Sixth Army and at least 500,000 men were involved on the Allied side alone. From Thiepval in the north to Estres on the Amiens–St Quentin road in the south, one could picture one continuous white curving line of smoke and bursting shells, slowly, creeping forward over a blasted country already kept under a bombardment by heavy howitzers for five or six days on end.

***

About noon, the brigade contact-patrol aeroplane came back with the first news of the assault for the anxiously waiting brigade staff. Guillemont was taken. Very soon afterwards, the first batch of prisoners came by in a long column. After them, the country was dotted with little groups of men, British and German indiscriminately mixed, some carrying stretchers, some walking singly and some in twos and threes, helping each other along. They were wandering on till they should come on a dressing station.

Presently an orderly appeared at the dark hole that led down to Brigade HQ with instructions for Pennycuick. Shortly afterwards he, Jackson and Holgate with Nos. 3 and 4 Sections disappeared in the direction of Trônes Wood. At about four o'clock, Smith and I followed with our sections.

The Bosch barrage was still falling on the front edge of Trônes Wood as heavily as ever. They didn't seem to have withdrawn many of their guns yet. In front, through the white smoke in the wood, we could see pieces of trees flying into the air. Once or twice a whole tree was lifted bodily upwards. The air was almost suffocating with the pungent smoke of exploding shells. It was impossible that the whole of our two sections and the 200 infantry who formed our working party could all get through. Some of them were bound to be hit. You couldn't stop once the long winding column of men were in the wood. The only thing was to go on and get through somehow.

It was dark by the time we got into Guillemont and there was nothing anywhere that one could recognise as a landmark. The details we had learned from the map to guide us were no longer there. It was some time before I even realised that we were actually on the site of the village.

Something had gone wrong. The 7th Division had failed to take Ginchy and our left flank was in the air. They were having another try at it with their reserve brigade but there was no artillery to back them up except perhaps half a dozen field batteries. The huge, complicated artillery machine had taken days and days to adjust and organise. When the time came, it could only follow out its programme blindly. If anything unexpected happened, a new programme could not be created at a moment's notice. The re-setting of the machinery could not be done in a day.

Jackson and Holgate were consolidating little scraps of trench out of the trench out on the flank towards Ginchy. We were to do the same on the east edge of Guillemont and construct strong-points to link up with the 59th Brigade on our right on the other side of the main street. There had been one small counter-attack already, and another was feared. The Irishmen were scattered all over the place and seemed inclined to fall back at the slightest thing.

We got to work where we thought the strong points ought to be and then I went off to the right to try and find anybody belonging to the 59th Brigade. At the bottom of a hollow, like a gigantic trench, which might be the sunken main road or might just as well be three or four 12- or 15-inch shell craters in line, I found one of Story's officers of the 96th Field Company, Formby I think it was. He was lost. He had been trying to locate himself for the last hour. He had been looking for the main road and couldn't find it. We decided after a little further investigation that the hollow must be the road we were looking for, and I went back.

The noise of the machine guns on the left towards Ginchy had died down, for the 7th Division had given up the attempt to make good that night. The Bosch shells, however, were coming with a steady 'crump, crump, crump' along the front edge of the village marked by three or four stumps of trees and were getting nearer and nearer to us. Every minute or half minute there was that slow, undulating and gradually increasing whine as a 5.9-inch [shell] came over and fell with a roar, sometimes short and sometimes just over our heads and into the centre of Guillemont. For the most part we were extraordinarily lucky.

As we dug, some evidences at least appeared which showed that this place of soft dark earth, pitted with conical holes intersecting each other, had once been a village with houses and streets. A few feet down, we unearthed the remains of the brick foundations, pieces of water pipe and splinters of timber from the roofs of the houses.

Every few minutes, a wild and excited, Irishman would appear out of the darkness, completely lost. He'd ask if anyone had seen such and such a company of the Leinsters or Connaughts. Nobody had, and he would go off again into the night, aimlessly wandering till he met somebody else to ask. If anything is calculated to produce despondency on a damp dark night, it is the brogue of a tired and excited Irishman. It seems to convey the very essence of all the hopelessness and desperation of men since the beginning of things.

At about midnight, the weather, which had been getting more and more threatening finally turned into a fine drizzle. Slowly the earth began to stick to the shovels, while little trickles of earth started to fall down at the sides of the rough trenches we were trying to dig.

***

During the next few days, we gradually got to know something of what had happened on 3rd and 4th September; of how the 5th Division on our right had had one brigade after the other wiped out in front of Falfmont Farm and failed to take it. There had been some misunderstanding between them and the French next door to them, and a gap in the barrage had been the result, or so the story went. We heard of how the 7th Division on our left had failed to take Ginchy and of how the 59th Brigade of our division had shot ahead as far as Leuse Wood while General Shute had sent back a message to the division to send another corps and we should be through. It was the grid at Guillemont Station that had been the deciding factor in the taking of Guillemont. The Bosch had watched it growing day by day and thought it was meant for a frontal attack on the trenches to the east of it, while in reality it was a system of assembly trenches for an attack southwards to take the village from the flank. It was all the work of the 20th Division, yet when we looked in the papers for an account of what the division had done (it was the first really prominent part we had taken in any operations) what did we find but a glowing account of how the gallant Irish Division had done the whole thing. Of course it was only done to stimulate recruiting in Ireland, but it was very hard on an untried and unknown division thus to have all the credit due to them usurped, especially by the Irish of whom no one had any but the smallest opinion.[76]

Chapter 7

LESBOEUFS (SEPTEMBER 1916)

6th September 1916

We pulled out from Carnoy on 6th September and marched back over the downs to Bray-sur-Somme. It was a beautiful morning, the first fine day after the wretched weather of the previous week.

Bray was just on the edge of the French area and all along the road was a continuous column of French troops and transport moving in the opposite direction. The whole population seemed to be sky blue instead of khaki. It was the first time we had really come into contact with the French and considerable interest was displayed on both sides. Apparently, they belonged to a new division which had just come up from the south and had never seen any British before.

French troops on the move are always impressive with their long coats and the ambling swing of their march. We were on the outskirts of another gigantic army, an army of blue that stretched down for hundreds of miles, division, after division, corps after corps. Here was another machine of a still more inconceivable size, the whole of another nation working alongside us with the same purpose against the same enemy. An organisation like ours and yet not ours. Everything of theirs, their equipment, their transport, their guns corresponded to ours and yet they spoke a different language and had a different point of view. They were French and we were British.

We got some billets of sorts in Bray and rigged up a mess in a bare, empty room that had been used as a billet for troops for years. There was nothing to do. We inspected the village and wandered down to the Somme – it was the first time we had seen it, except out of the carriage window in the train coming through Amiens. The French were everywhere. All the afternoon, columns passed and repassed, fresh troops and clean looking guns on the way up and dirty, ragged battalions tramping slowly back to rest.

Holgate turned up that evening from hospital – he had been gassed worse than the rest of us on the last night before the Guillemont show. Later on, the same day as we were having dinner (some curried bully and a few eggs we had been able to buy in the village) who should turn up but old Schon.

***

7th September 1916

The following evening, we marched on to Vaux-sur-Somme about 3 miles east of Corbie. The Bray–Corbie road runs along a hogback spur which separates the Somme and the Ancre as far as their junction at Corbie. You can look down to the left on the long, winding strip, some half a mile wide of swamps and lagoons, which constitute the Somme. In the dusk the river seemed very very far below, and across the deep gentian-blue patches of water – separated from one another by dark green rushes or grass or dotted with a little tree-covered islands – the steep hillside of the other side of the valley was just visible: a dark wall merging gradually into the evening sky as the downs stretched away and became flatter and flatter.

In places you could see the same kind of thing on the right also, across the valley of the Ancre, only here there was less water to be seen, and the valley was thickly wooded.

The valley of the Somme has the same features for the greater part of its length; steep chalk or limestone banks a couple of hundred feet in height flattening off at the top to bare undulating grass downs, dotted with little woods. At the bottom, the cliffs again flatten out leaving a strip of pasture, woodland or cultivation: anything up to 200 yards wide, bounded by the river road and beyond that the swamps and rushes of the river itself.

We had the main road to ourselves that evening and there was a silence such as we hadn't felt for weeks. There was only the old, homely and familiar sound of the company marching; the tramp of the sappers, the sound of the horses' hoofs, and the '*tock-tockling*' of the wagon wheels on the well-worn surface of the road. It was one of those times when the feeling came over one of what a wonderful thing a company of men was and how wrapped up in it we all were; when the company seemed more of an entity than the individual, when one's thoughts were merely a fragment of the company's thoughts. Each of us then had two pictures in our minds, side by side: the peaceful summer evening with the smell of the damp things by the river below, coming in little whiffs now and then. Next to it – almost superimposed on it – that other picture, not three days old, of the shambles before Guillemont. We dreamily compared the two as we marched along and wondered at the oddness of things.

Vaux is a typical little Somme village, nestling in a small hollow under the cliffs, a straggling cluster of houses of mud and wood along the river road. We got in at about ten o'clock and there were no billets for us. Very often there were no billets. We were only one of the odd units of the brigade group and whenever there was a shortage of billets, we or the trench mortar battery or the field ambulance had to go without. However, it was a fine night and we were out for a rest and everything had to be treated as a picnic. We slept in the open in a field of stubble just underneath the cliffs.

There was nothing to do the next day. We bathed in the river and lay in the sun resting. We felt as if we could live there all the rest of our lives. I went into Corbie in the evening with Schon and Jackson. It was the first place we had seen for over two months that had shops where one could buy what one wanted. There were no end of things to be bought for the mess. We had been living on bully, Maconochie[77] and biscuits for weeks past and had had no means of getting anything else. We bought as much as we could stow away in our pockets and saddlebags as there probably wouldn't be another chance before we went back into the line again.

***

8th September 1916

On the second day of our stay at Vaux, there was an inspection of the field companies in the division by the divisional general, [General] Douglas Smith. This was done on a bit of flat grounds near our bivouacs and was quite a short affair. He just wanted to congratulate everybody on the capture of Guillemont. We never knew him sufficiently well to appreciate how much the division owed to that tall old man who strutted about by himself with his hands behind his back. There was a general feeling, though, that he was a good fellow, and no one ever had a bad thing to say against him.

The question of the moment was, would Rolland ask him about the lorries and would he let us have them? Yes, the CRE was speaking to him and he nodded. Then the general rode away. 'It's alright', said Rolland, 'he's going to tell Colonel Dundas to order two lorries to be here at six o'clock tonight. There's room for three in my car too.'

That evening was a brilliant success. Everyone was filled with the joy of being alive. Rolland had organised a dinner at the Godbert in Amiens for all the officers of the divisional REs in celebration of Guillemont. We were all more excited and expectant than any children before a picnic, and the wild ride in the interior of a three ton lorry going at 30 miles an hour over the bumps of the main Amiens road put us in the right frame of mind to enjoy everything to the utmost as it came along.

The spirit of Amiens at that time was different to that of any other place during the war. I think it was the presence of the French army that made so much difference. A town in occupation by the British alone can never be gay in the same sense that Amiens was. One could feel it in the atmosphere almost before one dropped off the tail-board of the lorry.

The place was crowded to its uttermost. Never before had Amiens known such custom and such lavish expenditure of money or such crowds of men all bent on nothing but cramming every scrap of enjoyment into the a few short hours in which they were in the town. All the roads leading back from the 25 miles of battle front converged on Amiens, which lay like the apex of a great fan upon whose surface was concentrated all the available fighting strength of two nations. It was the great metropolis of that vast Anglo-French army, which could be counted not in hundreds of thousands but in millions and which was engaged in the most terrific battle of the whole war and of all history.

Of all the officers and men one saw in the streets, all the crowds in the restaurants and shops, representatives of every division, both British and French, that was not actually in the line, only a very minute proportion lived in the town. They had all come in for a few hours by jumping lorries and cars and would all depart again before the evening was over to their units twenty, 30 or 40 miles away. How they came or went was always a mystery.

Some belonged to divisions that had just been pulled out, like ours, for a breath of fresh air before being thrown in again for another battle. These were the divisions that had done well and hadn't had enough casualties to be allowed a proper rest. Perhaps only a few hours ago, some of these men had been up there, crouching down in the filth among the dead while the great green-backed flies buzzed angrily around waiting for more food; their battalions had been relieved at last, and they happened to be off duty. They jumped the first vehicle they could find going westwards and if it went in the wrong direction, out of it into another, sometimes waiting patiently on the road for an hour just to get an evening in Amiens. Imagine the dazed amazement with which they would suddenly find themselves in the brilliantly lit streets with shops stored with every article one would have expected to find anywhere in London before the war. Imagine the effect of the big restaurants like the Godbert with their merry crowds, their unlimited supply of wine and their wonderful menus on which the war appeared to have had made no mark whatever. Could it be true that they were the same beings who only six hours ago were away in that other world leading a life which had no single part in common with this?

Some belonged to divisions that had failed or that had lost very heavily: divisions that were divisions only in name, composed of skeletons of units whose few remaining members still lived with the memories of their missing friends, while the empty spaces at the mess table were filled with new faces who could never take the places of those who had gone. The whole country in front of and behind Amiens was full of these divisions. The worst could be sent away to some other part of the line as useless for further fighting, and the remainder would be 'fattened up' again. That was a new expression. It came in with some battle. It all seemed to be a question of casualty returns, worked out with a cold preciseness at [British] Army Headquarters at Querrieu by men who sat in offices and heard the war sometimes when the wind was blowing in the right direction.

Then again there were those whose battalions would be going back into the line next morning, probably for some new attack from which they knew the chances were against their ever returning. They were spending their last evening in civilisation.

It was the combined influence of this strange floating population that made up the peculiar atmosphere of Amiens. One could feel it everywhere, in the tone of the murmur of conversation around and in the very sound of the footsteps of the crowd in the streets; a sort of suppressed excitement, a wonder at the brilliance of the town and at the things displayed in the shops.

There were fifty of us that night, at table, in one of the private rooms opening into the great hall of the Restaurant Godbert including all the officers of the 20th Divisional Engineers. Stratton was there and all the Signals people and there were one or two battalion commanders from the 59th Brigade too.

It was a thoroughly good evening. Never can there be anything like it again, unless there comes another war and all the conditions are repeated once more. As the dinner wore on and the noise increased, the room began to fill from the main restaurant outside. Generals, staff officers, battalion commanders, and subalterns all streamed in, attracted by Rolland at the piano, and joined in the roar of the old songs that everyone knew. Inevitably the padres who had drifted in a little earlier thought better of it and departed.

In the final scene, towards midnight, before we were ejected by a combined force of waiters headed by the manager, I seem to remember a whirling mass of officers from which the red and blue armbands of divisional and brigade staffs appeared at frequent intervals, while the CRE performed an unsteady clog dance alone in the middle of a long table, among scattered plates and glasses. Suddenly there was a slight pause; four staff officers lined up and leaped upon the table in a row. There was a fearful crash which resounded above all the shouts and noise of the great restaurant, and the table collapsed in a heap of wreckage on the floor.

***

11th September 1916

We were on the march before dawn next morning, going east for the second time. The division was again on its way to the line and the whole 14 miles of it were crawling along the roads, each brigade group, like a long snake close to the right of the road to leave room for the unending stream of lorries, motorcars and troops crowding past in the opposite direction.

We halted at Méaulte and found some billets at the west end of the village, next to one of the new shunting yards that had thrust itself out on to the only bit of open space left in the valley, as the over-strained railways threw out more and more excrescences on which to try and clear the trains now standing end to end sometimes right back as far as Amiens, on the main line.

During the next few days the rumour began to spread that the great final attack was coming off. Something unusual was certainly going on. The Guards were in the line for the first time to begin with. The traffic on the roads was greater than we had ever seen it before and above all there were stray cavalrymen about and companies of motor machine gunners. It certainly did look like business.

It was on the afternoon of the 13th [September] that we got first news of something extraordinary. Pennycuick, Jackson and I were out for a ride, and we met Hobart and Brigadier Butler. Hobart was in a state of obvious excitement about something. Had we heard about them? He and the general has just been up to Loop Siding, along past the citadel to see them. Train loads of them were arriving. They looked like nothing else in the world – like toads perhaps.

None of us had the slightest inkling of them. Not a word or a rumour of any kind had leaked out. At Loop Siding on a level spot of the grass downs the clumsy canvas hoods had been lifted off them and they had crawled down out of the trains that had brought them there. A great new weapon with unlimited possibilities had suddenly appeared as if out of the sky. They were the first sixty tanks and had been hurried out from England in time for the attack the day after tomorrow, of which so much was expected. They were crude beginnings, but they were all the more grotesque and wonderful for all that. They had tails behind them, which made them far more like some strange animal than any of the later models.

They were drawn up in long rows and around them was a huge crowd of British and French officers in the little hushed groups into which people gather when some great new idea strikes them collectively. Another Wells story had come true. It seemed almost incredible that the secret should have been so well kept. Around each machine were four or five little blue-overalled mechanics with oil cans and cotton waste going over their charges after the railway journey like stablemen inspecting a newly arrived racehorse at the station. Now and then one of the machines would move forward and be taken for a little exercise.

That evening, the news of the Hush-Hush machines spread from valley to valley, and from camp to camp among the whole army waiting in billets, in camps and in bivouacs over the whole Somme country. The first suspicions of doubt as to the use of the whole colossal battle, that were just beginning to creep in with the first signs of winter, were all dispelled, and a vague thrill of expectancy filled everyone. At last something was going to happen. There were the cavalry all ready, and above all there were the tanks. This time there couldn't be any failure.

14th September 1916

Next morning, we marched by cross-country tracks, which had now almost dried up, to the Citadel Camp. Here again there was nothing for us but two old tents. There was a violent scene between Pennycuick and the old colonel who acted as camp commandant. He had apparently said something about the REs being expected to make shift for themselves and there weren't any more bivvy sheets to spare. Pennycuick had an uncontrollable temper and there were thunder and threatenings of reports to division on both sides.

I'm afraid I never hit it off very well with Pennycuick. The mess was very much anti-regular and always had been, and I had always been hot against the 'militarist' type of regular officer for whom nothing will do but the usages and traditions of the old army. In fact, I was prejudiced against all regular officers. We never thought of either Hopkins or Scott as regulars because they weren't 'militarists' and knew exactly how to treat the new army and to think with it. We had a great respect for old Hopkins. He treated us all as children and we never questioned, however incomprehensible his orders seemed. We had been spoilt by him I expect. Pennycuick resented my allusions to regulars and I resented being reminded of the ways of his old regular field company. We both had quick tempers too. It was a great thing to have Schon back. Wherever he was, there was an air of placid contentment that spread to everyone around him and overcame all difficulties. He was the one link, too, with the old happy days at Laventie. By this time he was second in command, White having gone to hospital with blood poisoning from a cut in the hand on some old barbed wire at Guillemont.

***

15th September 1916

The great battle of 15th September opened next morning with the most terrific bombardment. It was a general offensive along the whole front of the Somme. The last remaining points of the Ginchy Ridge were to be captured and the Allies were to flow down into the low-lying ground towards Bapaume. Apparently, there were no more lines of wire in front of Lesboeufs and Morval, so that the chance for the cavalry had come. They were to break through the 14th Corps front when the Guards and the 6th Division had taken the last line.

The 20th Division was in support and, like the cavalry, were waiting to follow through later in the day. At noon we got orders to move and five minutes later were on the march with just our sections and tool carts. All the heavy transport was left behind with Holgate. We dropped down into the Carnoy Valley just above Carnoy and finally halted at Talus Boise where the whole brigade group waited until nightfall for orders to move on. Just behind in the other branch of the valley were the cavalry: two Indian divisions and one British division. Everywhere there was great excitement. Next door to us there was a French balloon section with its lorry and telephonists. Every now and then a message would come down from the Frenchman up above and we pressed the old man at the bottom for news. Yes, Flers was taken. '*Une* machine' had been seen the other side of it. He thought Morval was taken too but he wasn't sure; he was chiefly concerned with the French front just to the south of Combles.

Why weren't we ordered up? Why was the cavalry still waiting? Surely, the Guards and the 6th [Division] hadn't failed. There wasn't a word of news. Night came on and the cavalry were still waiting – for the chance that never came, just as they had waited all through the war, at Neuve Chapelle, at Loos, and on the opening day of the Somme, two and a half months ago.

At 8.00 pm the inevitable rain came on and a cold wind blew up. It kept on all that night and we got colder and colder. Pennycuick and I shared a bivvy [sheet] consisting of a waterproof sheet supported by two sticks; the ends were open and the wind and rain drove in, soaking first our boots and then our legs and finally all of us, while gradually the water soaked in along the grass underneath.

16th September 1916

At 5.00 am we were on the march through the rain and mist towards Bernafay Wood. The cross-country track, now greasy with mud – like a continuous banana skin to walk on – led off to the east to meet the Maricourt–Briqueterie road and from there we turned north past the remains of the Briqueterie[78] and down into the valley of Trônes and Bernafay Woods where there were some old disused gun pits that might do to live in.

For the first time we were marching with our transport and all our belongings into the real desert country beyond the last vestiges of grass or any natural living things, into the country we had hitherto only known at night amid gas and bursting shells and lit up by gun flashes and looping Verey lights. There would now be no Carnoy to go back to in the early morning with its outlook of tree-lined roads and grassy slopes. As far as one could see in any direction there was now nothing: no picture upon which one could look to break the monotony of miles upon miles of brown earth, pock-marked like the surface of the Moon, with not a yard of undisturbed ground. The forward area in which we had, up to now, worked at night among the shells would now be the back area where we would spend the few hours of rest in between nights of work in a newly-created sea of brown craters further to the east.

But there were signs everywhere that the army was advancing. A broad-gauge railway line crossed the road near the heap of mangled steelwork that had been the Briqueterie – the road that we had only seen before as a slight hollow in the ground where decaying horses lay about in shell holes. It was where the field guns had been before. Now they were miles ahead, and their places were taken by great 9.2-inch howitzers, perhaps the ones we used to know away back at Carnoy. A little further on and one would have been fired at by machine guns; now a great locomotive stood against the skyline calmly blowing off steam.

We got some sort of accommodation near the north-east end of Bernafay Wood. Schon and I found a little place to sleep under two sheets of corrugated iron where one of the batteries which had taken part in the barrage during the capture of Guillemont had stored its ammunition. The rest of the company were scattered about in old gun pits and shelters nearby.

That night the 60th Brigade relieved the 1st Guards Brigade before Lesboeufs and at 3.00 am on the 17th Pennycuick, Jackson and I went up to reconnoitre our new trenches.

The great attack of the 15th had been a failure. It failed because the 6th Divisional commander had relied on two tanks to break down any resistance from the Quadrilateral, a little system of trenches just beyond his divisional front. The tanks never came, being knocked out on the way up or stuck in the mud, and the 6th Division as it advanced was mowed down by machine guns from the undestroyed trenches of the Quadrilateral. On their left and north of the Ginchy–Lesboeufs road, the Guards had advanced right up to the outskirts of Lesboeufs but had to use all their available men to form a long flank between them and the unfortunate 6th Division. Further to the left there was also a gap so that the line we took over from the Guards consisted of a piece of Bosch trench jutting out a mile towards the enemy beyond the rest of our line on the right and left.

***

The general direction of advance had been towards the north-east so that the French were now holding the Front due east of Guillemont and the only road that had enough metal in it to be worth repairing was the Briqueterie–Guillemont road, was now in their area and was used exclusively by them. In the whole of the 14th Corps area there were now no roads whatever running from rear to front. All the steadily increasingly traffic of troops, ammunition wagons, ration wagons, ambulances and guns were ploughing through the fast deepening mud of an improvised earth track which started from the road behind Bernafay Wood and ran along the bottom of the valley through Trônes

Wood and then up northwards, skirting round the north of Ginchy. (No one ever entered Ginchy itself or any other captured village until it was well out of range. They were always kept under heavy shell fire from the Bosch, who no doubt resented being driven out of them.)

Already after only a day and half's rain we saw ambulances stuck in the middle of the track, abandoned. It became impossible for an ordinary six-horse team to drag ammunition along and double teams of twelve horses had to be used to pull single half limbers through the mud by sheer force. No one was working on the track to improve it. There was nothing to be done. There was no road metal or even brushwood and thousands of tons of it would go nowhere on that track. It seemed that the cold unapproachable intelligences back at Querrieu and Montreuil had foreseen nothing of all this. Perhaps they had staked everything on a breakthrough. Did they know what conditions were like? We wondered if any of them had been up to see.

Even now there was a sort of expectancy left in the majority of people. There was a feeling that the Bosch was on the run or nearly on the run. There were no counterattacks now and his shelling, though still very heavy, was scattered and wild. He had lost the ridge and couldn't see. We were no on the top and he was some way down the slope towards the plain of Bapaume and Cambrai. In the last fortnight we had advanced further with each successive attack. There yet seemed a chance of breaking through. And yet, and yet, why were there no men working on the tracks to make them into roads so that the cavalry and tanks could advance? Every day we were going deeper and deeper into a roadless desert of mud. Surely, the staff meant to push on and follow the Bosch up. Oh well, it was no good thinking anything about it. If one didn't trust those mysterious people in motor cars and red hats who buzzed around the fabulous palace at Querrieu, what was the good of anything?

***

17th September 1916

It rained steadily all that night. After tramping for an hour and a half through the squelching mud that sucked boots at every step, we had only reached a point somewhere north of Ginchy. There were dead bodies lying about everywhere. In front, through the mist, occasional Verey lights showed up as vague luminous mounds of vapour that rose up out of the ground silently and fell again, lighting up against the blackness of the night the streaks of rain that were driving past our faces. There were shells bursting with muffled thuds over there on the right within the dim outline of tree stumps that marked the sight of Ginchy. They came whining over our heads one after another without a pause.

We were somewhere out on the top of the main Ginchy Ridge, though it was impossible in the darkness to see if the ground sloped up or down. This was the great ridge that had cost several hundred thousand casualties to capture in an intense battle lasting for nearly three months. How often had it been intimated in the papers that the object of the whole battle was to take this very ridge? What would they say now? There was no finality there. Those shells were still going over into Ginchy as if they would never stop. In the silences between, one could just hear the wind sweeping softly over the invisible sea of shell holes that stretched away in every direction into the night.

There was now no regular track at all, and we struck out eastwards hoping to find the Ginchy–Lesboeufs road. Every few yards there were dead guardsmen, officers and men lying anyhow in the shell holes. We stumbled over them in the darkness and they seemed to be giants of men. Raymond Asquith[79] must have been there somewhere I suppose.

Presently we found the road. It was merely a depression in the ground but it showed us where we were, and we followed it. About a thousand yards further on, to our amazement, there was grass growing on the sides: first little tufts showing above the loose earth scattered about, and then proper grass. The road too was improving. It was becoming a road – very battered and with huge craters in it – but still a road with metal left on it.

We were on the edge of the Promised Land. It was the first time since the beginning of the Somme Battle that troops had seen anything in front of them but brown shattered earth. The Guards had advanced on the 15th September, right out of the bombarded area, beyond the furthest limit of our barrage and had captured a little bit of the Gueudecourt Switch Line, which was still untouched by shells. Beyond was the open country with woods, villages and fields. Oh, if we could only follow it up and get them on the move before the Germans had time to make more trenches and new lines of wire in front of us.

Beyond the Flers Line, out in the extraordinary salient the brigade were holding, there were no shell holes at all. In their place was long rank grass or uncut crops and here and there, there were actually little patches of vegetable garden with cabbages growing. It was just a strip – a few hundred yards wide – of the Promised Land in front. A vision disclosed at intervals by the floating whiteness of distant Verey lights and seen through a curtain of driving rain; while all the time shells were bursting viciously on the road in front and behind and shooting out red-hot splinters into the darkness.

In a few days, no doubt, unless we advanced again, that little strip and the country for miles in front of it (in the vagueness of the other side of the Bosch lines) would be transformed by the ever-spreading brown blight and become merely a further portion of the sticky, undulating desert behind. Even now the 9.2s were coming gurgling over our heads and falling with dull thuds into and beyond Lesboeufs.

On the way back Pennycuick decided that we couldn't continue to live right back at Bernafay Wood as all our time would be taken in trudging to Lesboeufs and back along that impossible track. Brigade HQ had found a dugout by Guillemont Station and we thought we could probably find some shelter somewhere there too. Anyway, we couldn't stay back at Bernafay Wood.

17th September 1916 (continued)

We started moving house directly we got back from the line about 8.00 am. The rain had stopped and since there was no sign of any cover at all to be had, not even a bit of corrugated iron, we had to be content with bivvy sheets and a tarpaulin or two for the whole company and trust to luck that it would remain fine. All the remaining part of that day, until it was time to start out for the line in the evening, was spent by each man making some sort of a sleeping place for himself. Occasional shells fell about, so most people dug shallow holes in the ground (about 3 feet deep, like graves) in which to be protected from shrapnel and splinters. Two or three men shared a hole and laced their waterproof sheets together to form a roof. There was some difficulty in selecting spots to dig. Smith and I, who had combined forces, had several tries before we found a clean bit of ground that didn't exclude the acrid smell of rotten cheese, which is the natural guardian of bodies buried in the earth.

Towards evening the clouds got heavier again and time seemed drearier than ever before. A hundred yards to the south of us lay the splintered fragments of the train that had been caught by the guns in Guillemont Station. On the north ran Trônes Wood Track with its pathetic futility of teams of horses floundering in the sucking mud. The line of the track could now be clearly distinguished, as it wandered over the waist of brown, by a chain of broken-down wagons. The ambulance that had been hit that morning – and which we henceforth used as a landmark to find our bivouac – lay there a ludicrous-looking wreck, sinking slowly down. Behind was a dead tank at the bottom of a huge crater. It too was sinking and was now three quarters submerged.

Beyond these dismal landmarks there was nothing to be seen but the waste of mud that stretched as far as the dull water-laden atmosphere would permit one to see. And the winter had begun already. The land would never dry up again now. Troops by the hundred thousand were dotted about over the country, all cold, all miserable, and some … I thought of the guardsman we had found in the long grass near the Lesboeufs road in the early hours of the morning, who had lain there in the rain and cold for nearly three days, wounded in the back and half paralysed, but still alive and conscious. How many were there like him on whom nobody had chanced to stumble and who constituted a considerable portion of the 'missing' list.

It rained all night. We were digging assembly trenches just behind our front line facing Lesboeufs and at the same time reconnoitring to the north of the Lesboeufs road for a line to link up with the 59th Brigade. They were less fortunate and had no front line to speak of east of the Flers Line except two little bits of saps that ran out towards the Bosch.

The infantry of our own brigade were fairly comfortable. They occupied the old Bosch line along the whole of the brigade front. It was a good deep trench and there were deep dugouts in it, unfinished, staircases leading down some 20 feet or so. Here was one of the little things in which the superiority of the Bosch organisation struck us very forcibly. He must have been working feverishly on these dugouts just before the line was captured, and yet there was no spare material lying about, no tools, no dugout casing. We thought of what the place would have looked like if the British had been working there, of the sandbags, timber etc. that would have been lying about wasted, of the picks and shovels that the infantry would have thrown away over the side of the trench and left there when they had finished work.

Both on the right and left of the easternmost portion of our bit of line, the only part of the Gueudecourt Switch Line occupied by the British, the trench ran off across a sort of no man's land into the Bosch area and machine guns and bombers had been posted to keep any stray Bosch from coming up the trench. In the clump of trees on the road, there were known to be Bosch level with our line if not behind it. No one disturbed them, though, for the orders were to lie still and not attract attention. They apparently weren't sure where we were or how strongly we were holding on to the trench that jutted out into the lines for nearly a mile and we wanted to keep them in ignorance as long as possible. Once during the night we made out through the darkness a big party of them, perhaps a hundred strong, moving down the slope from Lesboeufs in the direction of the Quadrilateral. They passed by within a dozen yards or so of our line, probably a ration party or a relief who had lost their way.

After a two hour trudge, most of it from east of Ginchy onwards, through glue-like mud over a foot deep, we got back well after daybreak, very tired and soaked through, to our miserable camp, where we found that nearly all the holes we had dug for ourselves the day before were full of water. There was no dry place anywhere. It seemed as if there was no dry place left anywhere in the world. It was all brown and waterlogged and dreary. Towards the east, the white light of the sun, hidden behind the skirting clouds, shone down a long, irregular and speckled avenue of white formed by reflection from the little puddles where the water lay in the innumerable footmarks of men.

***

After that night we decided that of the two evils, an extra half hour's tramp added to each journey was better than having no shelter day or night from the rain and wind. A dry place, however small and for however short a time, was essential so we moved back to the old gun pits near Bernafay Wood. Here at any rate there were roofs of sorts and one could light a big fire without fear of being shelled. There was an outcrop of chalk here to which made a kind of oasis in the mud.

On the night of the 19th [September] the weather was more broken[80] and there were open spaces between the drifting clouds through which the moon appeared suddenly at intervals. We were still working on assembly trenches for the Guards to use in the next attack. The place seemed different that night. You could see further. Straight ahead in the moonlight stood the tower of Lesboeufs church not yet knocked down, and near it there was a little twinkly light, probably a candle or a lamp unmasked by mistake. It was like a night scene at a theatre. Again came the feeling that one was looking out at another world, separated by an invisible intangible wall, the thin boundary between the British and German lines. Then the clouds came over again.

We had a company of Durhams working with us. A new trench was being started and the men were all extended along the tape ready to begin digging. At the last moment one of us decided that the tape wasn't in quite the right place and moved it forward about 20 yards. The whole line of men with rifles slung and bayonets fixed followed the tape forward and at that moment the moon came out again. A green light immediately shot up from Lesboeufs, splitting into a shower of coloured lights. At the same time there came a wild burst of machine gun fire from the direction of the village. We all dropped flat on the ground and waited. In a few moments their artillery started and the air was full of red hot flying splinters, shrapnel and bursting shells. Luckily it didn't last long. Things soon got quiet again except for the usual shelling on the Lesboeufs road.

Of course, it was obvious what had happened. The Bosch was nervous and, seeing a line of bayonets shining in the moonlight and advancing towards him, had put up his SOS[81] for artillery support. The night before, the 59th Brigade had really attacked in an endeavour to improve their line, but beyond killing a lot of Bosch and getting very heavy casualties themselves, had done nothing much. The 59th Brigade had lost fairly heavily in the Guillemont show and hadn't had any reinforcements since. They were now down to about 400 men only, out of a theoretical 4,000.

***

On the 21st September, we were relieved by the Guards. They would take over the trenches as we had been digging through the nights of the last week. They would probably do an attack and there would be flaring headlines in the papers: 'Brilliant attack by the Guards' and an effusion by Beach Thomas. Then we should come along again and take over their line, consolidate it and prepare for another attack.

I think we were still rather proud of being kept in the 14th Corps with the Guards for so long. We certainly admired the Guards Division. They were a fine lot. Still in a way we resented them. They were naturally the favourites at a Corps HQ composed almost exclusively of Guardsmen. They were given every opportunity. They had their own channels for getting reinforcements and always got fully trained drafts – trained as they wanted them trained. They had longer periods of rest than we. Before 15th September, they hadn't been in the line since they left Ypres only a week or so after we did. Furthermore there were tales that they got the best of the rations, that they got more rum and when leave was going they got more leave. How much of it was true, I don't know, but that was the feeling. Given the same opportunities, we would be as good as they. We considered our division was as good as the Guards as it was, as far as actual fighting was concerned.

There was no particular joy at being relieved this time. We were all too exhausted to feel pleased or otherwise, and there was nothing to look forward to. At best it would mean a few days out only. We should march back for two days, probably be given the worst billets, or perhaps no billets at all at some dirty village for two or three days at the most and then back again to the mud still further to the east, still further away from shops and civilisation. And there was no prospect whatever of leave starting again.

***

21st September 1916

The night of the 20th was the last night of work and on the early morning of the 21st we tramped back to Bernafay Wood and from there straight on to the Citadel. The company just managed to drag itself in and slept until well on into the next day.

***

The Citadel was one of the great staging camps which lay dotted about the country in the zone of bare, undulating chalk downs between the desert country to the east of the old front line and the first of the inhabited villages further west.

In each corps in the army the divisions were in a continual state of rotation, some moving up towards the line and some moving back. No divisional troops could stop in one camp for more than a night or so for it would hold up the rotation. The whole country behind the desert area was divided up into these staging areas where brigades and divisions could halt for a night on their way backwards or forwards. Behind, the villages were grouped together into rest areas. The accommodation in the frail, insubstantial villages, composed of uncut poles and thin crumbling mud walls, was poor indeed. Sometimes it took three or more villages to hold a single brigade group. Every bit of accommodation, every billet as far back as Amiens and behind was packed with troops. As soon as one brigade group moved out of an area, another came in. If Corps Q made a mistake – as they very often did – a Brigade would be ordered into an area already occupied and there would be nothing for it but bivouacking, and this for battalions that had perhaps just come out of the line. Then an angry divisional staff would ring up 14th Corps and tell them what they thought of them and be baffled by the imperturbable voice of the Prince of Wales, who'd say he was very sorry and would see it didn't occur again.

Each corps had a definite back area in which to keep its troops, the front being divided up into corps sectors by arbitrary parallel lines, drawn by some authority at [British] Army HQ, reaching from the front line back for about 15 or 20 miles. It was generally arranged so that each corps area contained one road from rear to front (at least in the back areas; the higher command didn't seem to take much interest in the forward area). The 14th Corps area lay roughly along the valley running through Fricourt and Méaulte and then down the Ancre valley to Corbie. Our main road was the one running through Fricourt, Méaulte, Ville-sur-Ancre, Treux and Maricourt.

Along that road, during daylight, the 140,000 men of the 14th Corps were in continuous circulation. Divisions going up to the line would pass divisions coming back. Ten days was about the very longest that any division could stay in the line. Gradually, one got to know all the divisional marks on the transport of passing troops. Whenever any new mark appeared there was always a certain amount of interest to know what division had arrived in the corps and who they would relieve.

Every division had its own distinctive sign painted on every wagon and lorry in its possession. The sign of the 29th [Division] for instance was a flat red triangle and this was additionally worn by every man in the division. The divisional sign was one of the little things that did so much to foster *esprit de corps* in each division. There were multitudes of signs too besides the divisional ones. The divisional RE sign throughout the army was also a red triangle, like the Bass beer mark.[82] Each lorry column had its own sign so that the drivers at the back would be able to find the column again if it got split at a crossroads or level crossing. Then there were brigade signs and battalion signs in each division. In time, one got to know a great many of them so that one could tell at a glance a passing unit on the road, who they were and to what division they belonged.

***

22nd September 1916

After spending one night at the Citadel, we moved off again about midday through Méaulte and Ville[-sur-Ancre] to Treux. As usual the other side of the road was occupied by another division coming up. In both directions along the road the two columns stretched out apparently without end. This time, I remember, it was a division we hadn't seen before, the 17th. They were evidently coming up to take the place of the 6th.

That evening nothing seemed to go right. The first thing that happened when we pulled into Treux was that one of our drivers was dragged into one of the weed-filled lagoons by the mule he was watering and was drowned before he could be extricated. It was an unfortunate beginning to our day or two of rest and quiet. We then found that the comfortable mess which we had been allotted had been taken by the CRE of the 17th Division and we had to go around and search for some dirty little room elsewhere.

However, individual worries were very soon forgotten in those days. They never outlasted the actual day in which they occurred. We were in for three days' rest and after that we didn't know what was in store for us. We couldn't afford to think of either the past or the future.

Those three days later at Treux, from the 22nd to the 25th [September] comprised the longest consecutive period of rest we had been allowed to spend in one place since the fortnight at Calais five months before!

The happiness of those short bits of rest out of the line was something that one feels will never come again. It was the extreme contrast of feeling which nature provides to restore the balance and bring the general average of happiness up to its healthy norm. All the discomfort, fear and hopelessness of the last week was thrown off, and it was impossible not to enjoy every minute of the day. And yet there was no instant that wasn't commonplace enough, merely an afternoon at the tea shop at Heilly, a visit to one of the battalions in the next village, or a lorry jump into Amiens in time for dinner at Godbert or Josephine's. Yesterday was always forgotten and tomorrow was never thought of, except occasionally when its very uncertainty was smilingly brought up as an argument in favour of opening the third or fourth bottle of whisky in the day after a mild protest on the part of the mess secretary.

***

25th September 1916

On 25th September, the anniversary of the Battle of Loos, there took place the last great general attack of the Somme. From a newspaper point of view it was probably the biggest single advance that the British army had made since the beginning of the war.

On the 14th Corps front, in which we were chiefly interested, the Guards attacked from the trenches we had dug for them and captured Lesboeufs, while the 56th (London) Division on the right took Morval and so threatened Combles from the north. At the same time the French to the south captured Rancourt and Frégicourt[83] thus almost surrounding the Bosch in Combles. That night a continuous barrage was kept up on the bottleneck between Morval and Frégicourt in the hope that the garrison of Combles would be shut in till the attack was resumed in the morning.

Next day, Combles was definitely captured by the French and the 56th Division. The same day, after eleven weeks of repeated attacks and untold casualties, Thiepval, at the extreme north of the battle front, was taken at last. Except for the high ground at Sailly-Saillisel, the whole ridge from the Ancre to Péronne was now in the hands of the Allies.

As usual, marvellous stories and rumours reached us. We heard that the tanks and the cavalry were pushing on to Le Transloy and had reached the Bapaume– Péronne road without finding any Bosch anywhere. For two days we thought something big was going to happen at last. We had visions of rapid advance eastward, over and beyond the desert country and then open warfare and perhaps then the end of the war would draw in sight.

Then came a period of no news and with it the old doubts about the staff and their capabilities of ever being able to organise a real advance, even if the chance of one presented itself. Nothing was prepared. How could any transport manage to get through the miles of shell-pitted spongy earth with not a vestige of a road? And no attempts were being made to construct any. On all sides one heard the question asked seriously enough whether the Fourth Army staff had ever been anywhere near the forward area to see for themselves that there were no roads; to see for themselves the appalling conditions that were rapidly developing in the hundreds of square miles of loose brown earth as the water rose in the shell holes.

Chapter 8

'DEATH VALLEY' – GUEUDECOURT (SEPTEMBER–DECEMBER 1916)

During the two eventful days of 25th and 26th September we were on the march from Treux eastwards again via Ville Morlancourt, the Citadel and the Maltzhorn Valley to the southeast corner of Trônes Wood. We bivouacked here on a little space of bare ground between the remains of the wood and the main Guillemont road. We had a couple of tents with us which we had surreptitiously removed from the hoarded store of the fussy old camp commandant at the Citadel on the way up. There was considerable trouble, however, in pitching them for the shell holes were so close together that there was not a square yard of even tolerably flat earth between them.

Once again the one thing that struck us was the change in the character of the place since we had last seen it, the evidence that a steady advance had been going on.

Trônes Wood itself had altered little. There were the same ghastly relics – hanging in the trees and lying rotting on the ground – of the days, only three weeks ago, when it was not a wood so much as a dark horror through which it was just a matter of chance whether one came out alive. It was a little thinner now perhaps, but otherwise unchanged.

The road, however, which ran past eight and on to Guillemont was now one of the great arteries of the battle. All day long it was a seething mass of men and vehicles of all descriptions. Battalions on the march, both French and British. Stray tanks, still as much of a curiosity and far more thrilling than the first motor car to be seen in England. Caterpillars dragging the three sections of a 9.2-inch howitzer in an unwieldy train behind them. Guns of all kinds and wagons, blue and khaki. Anti-aircraft lorries, trench mortar batteries, road sweepers, motorcyclists, staff cars, and endless streams of ammunition mules.

Trônes Wood Station, just to the south of the road, was now in full swing, and sidings were growing and spreading along the roadside daily. A new development had appeared – the heavy Decauville railway with 9-ton trucks and steam locomotives. It was the culmination of the primitive little tramways with wooden rails that we had played with at Laventie and on the canal, still the same gauge, about nineteen inches. This, I believe, was the first system to be used by the British, though the French had used it for some time. Its base was Trônes Wood Station, on the broad gauge line, and it was to run forward to feed ammunition to the batteries along the Combles valley.

***

Very few things are more annoying than being shelled at night by a long range gun when one is sleeping in a tent. You are woken with a bang that seems to culminate some vague dream; you feel that something is wrong and that you are very high up in the air with nowhere to go for cover. The whistle and the bang come again, and you are very wide awake with that cold bright consciousness of a sudden awakening. Then comes the terrible dilemma: shall I get up or shall I go to sleep again? You get up and shiver in the silent starlit night. No one else seems to be moving. You go back to bed, only to be woken up again in half an hour's time when the same mental struggle goes on.

That night they shelled Trônes Wood fairly continuously, apparently with one gun that fired about every ten or twenty minutes. They didn't do any damage, but somehow one doesn't expect to be shelled in a canvas tent and one remembers the sensation of fear far more vividly than at other times when one is up and about and more or less ready, even though the shells are coming screaming down all round and death is really very close.

***

27th September 1916

We all went out the next morning to look round for a place for the company to live in which was tolerably close to the work we should be doing. The 14th Corps had sidestepped to the left, again to make room for the French, and the 20th Division's front was now from Gueudecourt to just north of Lesboeufs. We thought that perhaps we could find some old German dugouts on the Longueval–Flers road that might do.

Jackson and I went up to Flers, but there didn't seem to be any suitable place at all. We didn't like the look of the road either. It seemed to be a regular death trap. Twice we had a very uncomfortable time as shells came straight down the road in volleys from some Bosch battery that was enfilading it.

In a way that road presented a more revolting spectacle even than Guillemont Station. Very little remained of the actual road. Streams of ammunition wagons had been dragged over it, the wheels rolling from one shell hole down into the next and dragging the last vestiges of road metal with them. It was now just an uneven track, a foot or 18 inches deep in mud, and from the softer parts protruded pieces of wagons, field gun ammunition, and the bloated bodies of horses. It was along the sides, though, that the majority of the wreckage had been thrown, so as to clear the road itself for the unceasing stream of gunner wagons which still had to drive on. For over a mile there lay an unbroken column of shattered wagons with the six-horse teams sprawling about over the earth. They must have been there before the battle of 15th September, for the tanks had been long since on their way up to Flers. They had gone right over the bodies of men and horses: you could see their clumsy wobbling tracks all along, here across the stomach of a horse, there over two drivers. Sometimes they had ploughed through a pile of six horses in a shell hole, unable to avoid them. For the whole distance into Flers, it was as if cartwheels had gone over a road, covered with large tins of raspberry jam.

Smith had meanwhile been exploring Longueval and had discovered the entrances to several promising looking dugouts which the Germans had burrowed down underneath the debris of the houses. We soon decided that Longueval was the place to settle down, even though it was pretty far from the front.

Most of the 28th [September] was spent in clearing the dugouts of their litter of German junk – feather mattresses, straw, wine bottles and equipment. There were one or two of the late occupants still there in a very obnoxious condition and a good deal of chloride of lime had to be put down before their traces could be finally got rid of.

The tops of the stairs leading down to the different parts of our new home were all quite close to the road, in among the remains of the houses lining it. Just as we were congratulating ourselves, on our quarters, a battery of 8-inch howitzers arrived and settled down along the road within 50 yards of us. That evening they fired for the first time. All our candles went out, the plates jumped off the mess table and a shower of earth came down from a broken bit of mine-casing on the roof of the tunnel. However, we were certainly extremely lucky to have got hold of the dugouts. They had been there ever since the village had been taken over a month before and no one had discovered them.

***

30th September 1916

The 60th Brigade had not actually gone into the line yet, and so to fill up the time until we should be wanted for front line work, we were put on to clearing the remains of the Ginchy–Gueudecourt road as far as we could trace it and then levelling the shell holes to form an earth track up to Brigade Headquarters on top of the ridge.

We all knew it was a useless job and a waste of time, but it had been ordered and we had to do it. How was one to make a road to carry traffic of any sort without a scrap of road metal or anything? We did what we could. The worst and largest holes we stiffened up, after filling them in with earth, with a layer of old British and Bosch rifles and equipment that lay about everywhere. We collected all the shrapnel cases we could find and threw them in too, but it was all so childishly inadequate. Evidently no one was really bothering about the roads or how the troops were to get up to the line if it rained for any length of time, or the wounded be taken back.

***

Due north of Ginchy and east of Delville Wood there is a flattish hollow in the ground, about a square mile in extent, surrounded on all sides by rising ground, except to the northwest where a little narrow valley runs out towards Flers. On the south, the east and the north, it is bounded by the main Ginchy ridge and a long curved spur that runs out to the northwest. That hollow was the inaccessible centre, the Cranmere Pool, of all the desolation of the northern portion of the Somme battlefield. There were no living things there except men. Look where you would, there was no relief from the monotony of brown earth all of the same invariant shade. The surface of the ground was quite uniform – just one huge shell hole after another and to walk about, it was necessary to thread one's way along the narrow crests between them. If you slipped, you slid down 7 or 9 feet into the softest, spongiest earth it is possible to imagine.

The weather was bright and clear again, and the surface of the earth was dry. There were no beaten tracks and consequently there was little or no mud. Down at the bottom of the holes it was damp. At this period the water had not yet appeared above the earth. The original holes, of course, made by the exploding shells were twice as deep and their surface was compressed into a firm wall through which no water could soak away. On the top of this, all the loose earth that had been hurled into the air had settled. All the time, water slowly collected underneath; presently it would appear at the bottom and each shell hole would become a sucking bog.

One could get accustomed to the dead that lay about everywhere in all the stages of decomposition, some fresh, some so bloated that you would think their clothes would burst open. One came to walk round by the windward side of a dead horse almost automatically. But the strangeness of that desert country was a thing one could never quite get used to. It was the idea that all this has been done by the hand of man as a necessary means of killing his enemy. Only a month or two ago this country was smooth and cultivated, the peasants were living in Ginchy with their families, and old farm wagons trundled along roads that were now untraceable. The artillery had done all this and a hundred square miles of it besides.

They were at it still. All round the inner slope of the semicircular ridge were little dark objects that intermittently produced a green flash and a puff of pale white smoke. Hidden from the enemy by the ridge were concentrated all the field guns of all the divisions of the 14th Corps, battery after battery, brigade after brigade, each gun dumped down a shell hole and roughly screened from aeroplanes by wire netting with strips of cloth woven into the meshes. When they fired, the shells just skimmed the ridge and went sailing out into the Bosch lines down in the plain of Bapaume.

Sometimes as you watched, a great uncouth thing would get up out of a crater where it had been mending itself and crawl away out of sight. It was just the sort of thing one unconsciously expected to see. It fitted in with the general scheme of things, a strange new thing that had never been seen before, inhabiting a strange new world.

***

2nd October 1916

It was while we were engaged and clearing away the earth and dead Bosch from the Ginchy–Gueudecourt road that I first came in contact with any Signals people outside our own divisional signal company.

We were told that some dugout had to be made for 14th Corps' Signals, and an officer came up to explain what he wanted done. We had never heard of Corps Signals before, in fact we hadn't ever thought about there being any other signal people besides the divisional signal companies. We had, of course, always known the three brigade signal officers of the 59th, 60th and 61st Brigades. Sometimes we chaffed them about living in the comfort and opulence of brigade headquarters, sometimes we groused to them about the tangle of wires along our trenches. In quiet times we were able to induce old Brace to give us a telephone and Stratton was a familiar figure in his little car or trotting around Divisional Headquarters. Beyond them we took no interest in Signals.

This officer was an interesting phenomenon. It was evidently the first time he had ventured up as far as Longueval. He had a map with him and we gathered that his colonel who lived at Corps HQ wanted to bury a lot of telephone cables in the ground from somewhere at the back past Ginchy and out to the ridge in the direction of Lesboeufs. They wanted us to make a series of deep dugouts for them to use as test points where they could lead local telephone lines in and join them to the main buried route. We were quite interested in it all.

Next day, an aged corporal and a couple of men and an officer arrived in a box car. We all went off to see where the officer wanted the dugouts. We got to the sick-looking road we had been working on and he took out his map. He had apparently been told to put the dugouts a certain distance from another road marked on all the maps, but now non-existent. I suggested he showed me the direction he wanted the bury to go, but he didn't know the country and hadn't got a compass. He was evidently very much at sea. Just then a salvo of 5.9s came over and burst about a hundred yards off. They were having a shoot at one of the batteries. He was in a great hurry to be off and I believe he finally settled on the positions for the dugouts quite at random. The corporal who was to take charge of the cable burying had apparently never been outside corps headquarters before. However, that was their look out.

We soon got to work with the dugouts, C Section, working in reliefs all the twenty-four hours. The next night an enormous crowd of infantry appeared, a whole battalion. We had to assist considerably in getting them to work digging the cable trench as the signal people had never handled a working party before and a whole battalion takes a little setting to work if they arrive all at the same time, and if it is a dark night. That I believe was the first serious attempt at a buried cable system to follow up an advance that the British Army had ever made.

We were probably far too critical than was fair of the efforts of 14th Corps Signals. Still, it amused us at the time.

***

4th October 1916

On the 4th October, the bad weather came on again and within a few hours the mud began. The 60th Brigade were going into the line that night and we had to send out parties to lay tape lines from Ginchy up to brigade headquarters on the top of the ridge. There were no beaten tracks and without some guide it was impossible to find one's way through the shell holes and through the field gun lines at night.

The same day we got orders to start work on new assembly trenches and dugouts just north of the Miller's Son crossroads in preparation for another attack. We started out fairly early in the afternoon so as to get as much daylight as possible for the march up. It was a long way and we weren't sure how bad the mud was, or how long it would take.

From Longueval we went due east, skirting the southern edge of Delville Wood and along the line of tree stumps that marked where the Longueval–Ginchy road had once been. We then turned northeast past a dead horse that was by now a familiar landmark (by day and night), across the Ginchy–Flers road that we had previously been working on, and up the slope of the ridge, threading our way carefully through the field gun lines to brigade headquarters on the crest. Here we waited for our working parties of Durhams.

Looking northwards from the ridge, the ground falls away to Bapaume, the church towers of which we could just see, shining in the evening sun. The whole plan of Bapaume was spread out like a map. On the left we could see the Albert–Bapaume road, with its avenue of trees running in a perfectly straight line towards the cluster of white steeples in the distance. Straight ahead, between us and Bapaume were the villages of La Barque and Ligny-Thilloy and as we watched, first one little puff of white smoke appeared among the houses, and then another till, in a minute or two, both the little villages were lost to our sight in a heavy bank of white and pink smoke that slowly drifted away to the west in a long low cloud.

On the right there was a similar long, straight tree-lined road running towards Bapaume with little clumps of trees around the villages of Beaulencourt and Riencourt.

None of that country in front was ours. None of those little shady villages that had as yet been hardy touched by the guns. They all still belonged to the Bosch. There was now a rumour that the battle would go on all the winter. Even so, we should never possess those villages. They would crumble into dust and mud as we advanced and those fields around them would become one with the ever-growing desert of brown holes behind us.

Presently the Durhams turned up and we started off down the hill towards the line. Our way lay down a little narrow valley between two small spurs leading off the ridge. The division we had relieved had called it 'Death Valley' and the name stuck. As it got dark, the inevitable low whining began and *'whump, whump, whump'* came the shells on either side of us. The valley was getting narrower and deeper and any moment, they might begin to search the bottom where our path lay. Sometimes a stray shrapnel would come over and burst overhead; sometimes a salvo of 5.9s would burst with a quadruple crash on one side or the other. Yes, there they were, four big shells bursting right across the valley just 50 yards ahead. Then four more and some shrapnel behind. What a long way it was to the crossroads.

Once past the Sunken Road, things were fairly quiet that night. The Durhams were wonderful diggers, and we got along with the work very well in spite of the rain that kept on steadily all night. Coming back, it took an hour to reach brigade headquarters on the on the top of the ridge. The ground was like ice, with fresh washy mud and it was almost impossible to keep one's footing going uphill.

We parted with the Durhams at the top of the ridge. They lived in the old Bosch trench that ran along quite close to brigade HQ. It was pitch dark. We envied them living there close at hand, while we still had an hour's tramp on through the blackness. We saw the two officers drop down into the trench and disappear into an old German dugout from which issued a momentary warm red glow as they drew aside the blanket over the entrance.

We were soaked through and it was still pouring with rain. I pushed off down the slope in something like the right direction. It was impossible to walk in a straight line for more than two paces together, so even a compass was useless. One had to thread one's way this way and that, along the ridges between the holes. Every minute or so, a particularly bright Verey light – far away at the front beyond the ridge from whence we had come – would make a quivering glow in the sky and enable one to make out vaguely from the configuration of the ground more or less where one was. At every step at least one of the men behind would slip and slide down the sticky side of a shell hole. However, we were on the way home and there was a tot of rum waiting... and then a good sleep.

There was a faint smell of gas in the air, but I hoped it was only some old gas lingering in the ground. No, it was getting stronger. The Bosch must be gas-shelling our own batteries, which were quite nearby now. There must have been dozens of our own field guns ahead of us in the darkness, hidden down in old shell holes, and all pointing more or less at us. The body of a sapper belonging to the 84th Field Company had been found one morning recently in front of a British battery, with a hole through him where an 18-pounder shell had gone!

The smell of gas was getting stronger and we heard them coming over our heads and falling with an almost inaudible '*phitt*' in the ground. Damn the gas shells. We pushed on as fast as we could. Our hands were long-since caked with cold wet mud from repeated falls. One or two men began to cough – it was getting uncomfortably strong. Suddenly I ran into something solid sticking out in the darkness. It caught me in the stomach: a post or something. I put my hand out and felt something warm and round. It was the muzzle of a field gun.

***

5th October 1916

At four o'clock in the afternoon we started off again to carry on with the work. I went on with the assembly trenches, Jackson and his section were engaged in building a dugout for the brigadier, and Smith and Holgate were working on dugouts for first aid posts and for Battalion HQ about a hundred yards behind the Sunken Road. We got back about 6.00 am and slept till midday.

6th October 1916

We went out again that evening at about 5.00 pm to finish the preparations. They were dropping some more gas shells in among the field guns behind the ridge as we went past, but we managed to skirt round the area where they were falling. Otherwise, things were very quiet. The attack was to have been that evening at 6 o'clock, but for some reason or other it had been postponed till the following day. The Bosch, however, had by some means or other got wind of the original hour it was fixed for. Promptly at 6.00 pm, just as we got up to the Miller's Son, he opened a barrage right along the Sunken Road. We dashed on and managed to get to the trenches we had been digging without any serious casualties. Once in the trench there was comparatively little danger, unless a shell happened to fall right on the top of one. It was only a field gun barrage. In less than half a minute all the tiers of British guns behind the ridge had opened up and were replying vigorously. The whole black outline of the ridge appeared out of the darkness, silhouetted against a flickering greenish yellow glow of gun flashes. In front, the Germans were now sending up rockets and Verey light signals of all kinds and colours. We waited, crouching down at the bottom of our trench. We weren't quite sure what it all meant. Perhaps the Bosch were going to attack.

After about twenty minutes, things began to die down and nothing remained of the gun flashes except the slow, irregular firing of some battery of big guns, which had probably been going on unconcernedly the whole time, firing at some distant target quite regardless of the commotion in front.

***

7th October 1916

Next day, the 60th and the 68th Brigades attacked at 2.00 pm in conjunction with the 12th Division on the left and the 56th (London) Division on the right. Two hours later the situation was still rather obscure when Pennycuick, Smith and I went forward from Brigade HQ where we had been waiting. We were to ascertain what the position was and to settle what was to be done in the way of consolidation during the night. Jackson and Holgate were to follow with a working party of 200 Shropshires as soon as it got dark enough. The brigadier had sent orders for a further 300 men from the 12th KRRs to meet them at Battalion HQ near the Sunken Road.

The objective had been the second German line in front of Le Transloy. It meant the capture of the crest of a slight rise in the ground which overlooked the village. As we passed the Miller's Son, the usual hour or two of comparative quiet after an attack was just being broken by salvos of Bosch 4.2-inch howitzer shells, which were falling round about the neighbourhood of the crossroads.

The 12th Rifle Brigade – who with the Oxfordshire and Buckinghamshire Light Infantry were actually engaged in the attack as far as the 60th Brigade was concerned – had their headquarters in a German dugout in the side of the Sunken Road. All round, there was a confusion of stretchers and wounded men limping about. There was nowhere to put the wounded. There was absolutely no hope of getting them back that night. It took five hours to carry a stretcher back to Ginchy, which was the nearest point where the roads were good enough to get even a horse-drawn ambulance. Wounded still kept coming down from the new front and collecting aimlessly, and the shells were coming over in increasing numbers.

From there on the grass appeared, and the ground was not very much broken up by shellfire. The night was clear, for a wonder, and there was a moon a few days old. Bosch machine guns kept starting up in the little bursts and traversing across our path. At last we caught sight of the new front line in the moonlight ahead. In a long line behind the trench were the bodies of the Bosch who had been shot or bayoneted and flung out of the trench. There were bodies of Rifle Brigade men too in almost equal numbers, but they were all scattered about in the open behind. There was only one officer left in the RBs of those who had taken part in the attack. He was a South African called Ruddle: one of those stout-hearted men who were always drunk when out of the line and always did wonderfully well in any show, and who never seemed to get hit.

The German trench was good and deep as far as it went, but it was only about a hundred yards long. We had to find where the flanking brigades were and try to join up with them so as to form, as nearly as possible, a continuous trench. For nearly a quarter of a mile on each side, there was nothing but a series of hastily scratched holes with a couple or so of men in each.

Meanwhile the shelling was getting steadily worse. A stream of shells was whistling over our heads and falling on the track we had come up. Thank goodness they hadn't got the range of the front line yet. They were firing over. The rest of the company with 400 infantry ought to be arriving any time now. Poor Jackson and Holgate. They must be having a rotten time away back there in Death Valley or crossing the Sunken Road.

At last, a long, dark winding column appeared in the moonlight coming up from the rear. Jackson was leading. He, Pennycuick and Smith went straight off to the left with the Shropshire party and I picked up the KRRs and Sergeant Pegg with my section, which seemed extraordinarily small, and went off to the right to join up with the 56th Division.

It was a difficult job getting the men out and their jobs allotted. There was only one infantry officer with them, and he was a youngster who had just come out from England. The others had been knocked out on the way up. The moonlight was very clear and we must have showed up against the skyline, for the Bosch started machine-gunning and sniping almost immediately. The rain of shells coming over our heads was growing into a regular barrage. They were bound to shorten the range before long. However, Pegg told me they ran right into it in Death Valley on the way up. The two companies of infantry had eighty men, and half the officers were knocked out. One shell had landed right among the sappers, blowing Sergeant Yule of No. 3 Section literally to pieces and killing or wounding ten sappers of whom six belonged to our section.

The moon went down sometime before midnight, leaving a dim murky greyness lit up by yellow flames that leapt from the ground behind us on both sides – now here now there – in an unending succession, as the shells kept falling about. The air was full of loose earth and mud, heavy and acrid with the gases of exploding shells. Great pieces of metal came hurtling by with a harsh vibrating buzz as the jagged edges went tearing through the air.

It seemed impossible that anyone could live through this until morning. It was the only time I can remember when I really felt I shouldn't ever get back again. Now and then one of the sprawling Bosch bodies on the ground would move and groan, but no one paid any attention. The sooner they died the better. There was no hope of their being got back.

More than once I was knocked down either by the force of a shell or by great lumps of flying earth. Shells were dropping everywhere now. One couldn't distinguish any individual ones coming through the air. The work was going on very slowly. Unless Sergeant Pegg and I were constantly on the go backwards and forwards along the top of the trench, the infantry would stop digging and crouch down at the bottom.

Suddenly there was a shriek, and a blazing yellow flame that seem to fill the whole universe. Then everything began to spin round with a great singing noise, and I found myself lying on the ground with a rain of hot earth still falling on me. I picked myself up and went on. There was a great noise in my head and a curious indifference to what happened to me. The shells bursting all round seemed to mean nothing. But I was terrified that something should happen inside, that I should suddenly run away into the darkness.

A few minutes later I came across Ruddle again. He was just the same as ever, cheery and apparently quite unperturbed. He had just been going through the pockets of a dead Bosch officer and found a flask of whisky.

***

Somehow or other we got back to Longueval in the early morning. Everyone was just about finished. I remember pouring out a tot of rum for Smith in the dugout. He drank it, collapsed on the floor and slept without moving until well on into the afternoon.

I woke up at about four o'clock and remembered we were going back to rest next day. Thank God we shouldn't have to go out again another night. Then at nine o'clock in the evening there came a message to say that the 12th Division (the flank division of the 13th Corps on our left) had failed to take Gueudecourt and that Cavan had ordered the 61st Brigade to put up some wire round their left flank as there was a gap in the line. The 84th Field Company had already gone back to rest and there was nothing for it but for us to go up again and do the job for them. It was about the last straw. We were all so tired. Anyway, it had to be done so it was no use grumbling. A carrying party of infantry had already been ordered to go to Guillemont and fetch up wire and stakes etc. but it was very doubtful if they would get the stuff up to the line in time to get the job done by daylight. And we had been dawdling over dinner down in the narrow tunnel with the broken roof – a dinner of Maconochie, ration biscuit and whisky, thinking silently about not having to go out into the darkness and shells afterwards!

At ten o'clock Smith and pushed off up the road to Flers. The mud stank revoltingly and in the light of each gun flash there were horrible things sticking out of it. We waited in the 61st Brigade mess. There was no one else there. The General had gone to bed and Finken, the Brigade Major, was in his office further down the tunnel. Outside it was raining again. Now and then, orderlies came and went, their boots squelching in the mud.

I had never felt so despondent before. There was nothing ahead to look forward to – absolutely nothing. The last spark of the expectation and vague excitement that we had at Guillemont, and even later in front of Lesboeufs when there still seemed a chance of a real advance, had died out. The winter had come now. There was no chance of the war being over for years. And there seemed no chance of leave.

I remember something that young Musters had said a couple of weeks ago, in that curious strained voice of his:

> Why are we still staying on in the Division? All the fellows we knew have been killed or wounded. I hardly know a soul now. Who is there left of all the old Laventie crowd? It's funny how a few here and there stay on and never get hit or go to hospital or anything. It's time those polished gentlemen behind were weeded out and sent up here to take our places.

Why had I never been wounded or gassed? Those ten fellows in my section who were hit last night were all men just out from England. Most of them would go back again now. They'd have a rest in hospital and people to look after them. And they weren't entitled to a rest. They were fresh to the life others of us had been leading for months and months. When they heard a shell, it couldn't mean anything to them except a vague sense of danger. They had seen nothing of all the horrible scenes shells could produce.

How many of the old section, the old Laventie section were left now? I could count them on my fingers. Seven. Seven out of thirty-two. And Perrin and I had been counting up the total number of casualties there had been in the section: thirty-eight. And last night's ten made forty-eight. Nearly 130 per cent.

Yes a few seemed to go on and on. One's nerves would surely go in time, gradually, gradually, until – what would happen? No one cared. There were instances one knew of – many of them: of self-inflicted wounds, of desertion and of complete mental breakdown. Musters was right. Why shouldn't we change places with those wretches at the back? Let them come and see what was going on at the Front while they were drinking and playing cards in St Omer or Calais, enjoying a happy pre-war existence, free from the worry and monotony we suffered.

We had been down in the Somme longer than any other division. From all accounts the rest of the division was going back for a rest for a time and then returning again to the impossible roadless mud of a winter on the Somme. If the division did go back to Amiens, we engineers might not go with it. The field companies could be kept in the battle area and given various jobs, which – like every other job we were given – we would be expected to finish.

***

The carrying party with the wiring materials didn't arrive until it was too late to start work that night, so the brigadier sent us back sometime about three in the morning.

9th October 1916

The division *was* [editor's italics] being relieved. We slept for a couple of hours and then packed and marched off back to the crossroads just behind Bernafay Wood. We were told that somebody would be sending lorries. We waited from nine o'clock until one, but none appeared. 'Somebody' probably hadn't remembered to order them. Then a little train appeared on the metre-gauge railway – which the old French sappers had been mending – through a clearing in Bernafay Wood. We talked to the French driver. Yes, he was going back to Albert and could take us back, nearly as far as Méaulte.

It was still raining and the Sandpits Camp was all sticky with mud. This was the place where we had stayed on our first night in the battle area; this was where we had seen the mushrooms of smoke on the skyline and been thrilled that we were actually going to take part in the battle. What a difference there was between then and now. It had been brilliant summer then and everything was filled with bustle and excitement. It was all so new to us. Now it was winter, and everything was dull and wet and heavy. We were dead tired and strung up and there was nothing to look forward to. The whole division was tired out. The battalions were all down to a couple of hundred men. Nearly all the old officers were gone. The whole aspect of the war had changed.

***

For the next three days we did nothing except clean up, check stores and kit, see to the horses and send back to Corbie and the EFC[84] to replenish the mess with food and whisky. We had had nothing but rations for weeks.

13th October 1916

Then there was an inspection of the 60th Brigade Group by Cavan on the downs between the Sandpits and 14th Corps HQ. It was the first time the whole brigade had been together on parade since it had come out from England originally. Cavan made a speech and told us all about what a fine brigade the 60th was and how wonderfully well the 20th Division had done and that he wouldn't ever let it leave the 14th Corps. He said he'd rather have the 20th under him than any other division in France except his own Guards. He also promised us good billets near Amiens.

Pennycuick left the company the next day. He had been chasing hares on the downs with the brigade staff and had come off his horse and broken his jaw. Schon was now acting OC [of the] company.

That afternoon we got orders to march back to Daours on the Somme between Corbie and Amiens. At the same time a message came from division to say that there was an allotment of special leave for us: one officer and three 'other ranks' were to proceed on leave the next day. It was my turn.

At 3.00 am we were jogging along the road into Amiens in a limber to catch the train for Le Havre.

***

2nd November 1916

It took four days to get back from England to the company. It was the same old thing. How we did hate those RTOs at the stations. At that time none of them had been to the front. They were '*embusques*'[85] who had got soft jobs at the back yet treated us like dirt. They never knew where one's unit was and sent one careering about the country for days, from one miserable railhead to the next, getting colder and colder in freezing carriages with broken windows and often no doors.

The staff on the railways were the only kind of staff officers behind our own divisional and brigade staff whom we had come into contact with. In our eyes they typified the whole of the Staff in the rear and there was bitter feeling against them.

It was a feeling, I suppose, very much like that at home between the very poor and the very rich. How often did one see an officer returning from leave, trudging back to his unit along the road and hailing a passing staff car – containing only one young man with blue tabs lying back luxuriously under his fur rug – only to be splashed from head to foot with mud and left to shake his fist in pathetic rage at the retreating staff cap.

I eventually found the company at The Craters, near the old front line between Carnoy and Montauban, where a large-sized camp had sprung up built of new Nissen huts which had just been introduced. We had one as a mess, which we shared with the field companies of the Guards Division.

Our work consisted of putting up more huts and laying a 6-inch pipe from Montauban to Guillemont.

As usual the main part of the division was still 'at rest' in the smiling country behind Amiens. We [engineers] were up working. However, we were fairly comfortable and made the best of things. In the evenings the chief amusement was smoking rats out of their holes with lighted cordite and shooting them as they came out.

***

8th November 1916

One evening a huge red glare appeared to the south-west, somewhere in the direction of the Somme, miles behind the front. Then we heard a curious crackling noise, and now and then the red glow would increase into a great flash, to be followed after nearly a minute's interval by a rumble of explosions. It must be miles away, and yet it sounded like just over the hill.

It went on all through dinner, until there came a flash which seemed to fill the whole sky with red lightning. Then after seemingly minutes of waiting, the whole roof of the semicircular tin hut bulged in visibly under the impact of probably the biggest detonation that had ever occurred.

We heard afterwards that it was the great French ammunition dump at Chipilly on the Somme. Field gun ammunition by the 100,000 in wooden boxes had been set on fire by an aeroplane bomb, and had gone on blazing away with small explosions until the intense heat had finally detonated the main dump of acres of big shells.

***

11th November 1916

On 6th November, Captain I.W. Massie, who had been Adjutant to the CRE, arrived to take over command of the company and on 11th November we handed over work on the pipeline to another company and moved back to billets at Ville sur Ancre. From there we moved on to Corbie on the 15th where we rejoined the 60th Brigade Group. We remained there until 9th December, working on the building of a divisional cinema, divisional baths and laundry etc.

9th December 1916

We were ordered up again for work under the chief engineer [of] 14th Corps. There was no accommodation for us, so we had to dump ourselves down in the mud and old shell holes between Trônes Wood and Guillemont. We built a camp of little shelters made of two low sandbag walls, spanned by curved corrugated iron sections. There were no roads leading to the camp and our horses had to be picketed in the mud into which they sank about a foot on the first day.

***

During the time we had been away, the first trench-boards had begun to arrive, so two of our sections were employed laying a track over what was now a watery swamp of shell holes, half full of water from the final end of metalled road at Ginchy up to Lesboeufs. So deep was the mud that each 6 foot length of slatted wood had to be supported on piles driven down into the clay. It was a sort of causeway over the shell holes a couple of feet wide. Soon, when the first sharp edges of wood got worn off, it got so slippery with mud that one couldn't keep one's feet, so every bit of board had to be covered with wire netting or thin expanded metal.

With the continuous rain, the water was rising ever higher in the shell holes and movement was becoming impossible except along trench board tracks. One could only get across country by walking around the narrow rims, zig-zagging between the holes – anything from 10 to 40 feet wide – each with its rising lake at the bottom and its sloping sides of half liquid clay. So many parties of men had to move backwards and forwards to and from the front line (reliefs, water carrying parties, ration parties, gunners and stretcher bearers) that every possible winding track above water was being tramped into mud, feet deep. Men struggled about like flies caught in fly paper.

Individuals who lost their way at night and slid into one of the shell holes were seized by the clay and sucked down in spite of all their struggles and slowly drowned in the icy mud. If a man got in to the muddy water, even up to the waist, it usually took a party of men an hour or so to get one out. Things got so bad that eventually an order was issued that no one was to go about alone and that all parties must carry a drag rope with them.

It was getting harder and harder to get materials up. Something had gone wrong with the railways: rolling stock had been allowed to drift up to the forward railheads and couldn't be got back fast enough, so that mountains of stores were collecting at the bases. It was at this time that Eric Geddes[86] was sent for, in desperation, to put things right.

Chapter 9

SIGNALS (DECEMBER 1916–AUGUST 1917)

19th December 1916

On 19th December, my transfer to Signals[87] came through. I was to report to OC GHQ Wireless Company at Hesdin near Montreuil. The next day I arrived there and started immediately on a five week course of wireless [communications].

It was a queer place. The war was very far away. In the mess everyone talked wireless technicalities all day long. Nothing else mattered. It was their hobby and they were all wrapped up in it. However, it was all very interesting and very different from the trenches in front of Lesboeufs!

There were about five other officers like me learning wireless, and about sixty other men: German-speaking interpreters of all nationalities, being taught the art of listening with amplifiers to Bosch signal messages up in the line. They were taught by one Classe, a professor of music. There were lots of officers in the mess. It seemed to be a sort of depot of wireless officers. Then there were a lot of very civilian officers with long hair who were allowed to dabble with army wireless equipment, presumably for their own advancement when they got back to civilian life. It was a very pleasant war for them.

Just before Christmas it got very cold and snow fell; then that extraordinary frost began, which lasted nearly all the winter.

***

24th January 1917

On the 24th January, I was posted to the 14th Corps Wireless Section and left in a box car[88] for 4th Army Headquarters at Querrieux. I arrived nearly frozen. Next morning, I saw Colonel Earle, the AD[89] Signals of the 4th Army, and then went on to 14th Corps Headquarters at Méaulte, reporting to Colonel Mordaunt, the AD Signals. Finally, I proceeded up to Maricourt near Carnoy, where the other wireless officer, Newcombe, was living in an old French dugout.

It was a good dugout and Newcombe had an oil stove, and in a short time we were very comfortable. It was very lucky [my] being able to get back to the same corps again. I knew the country and one had friends around.

The work consisted of looking after a series of trench wireless stations along the corps front and also a couple of listening sets for which we had a special section of interpreters. They were a queer collection: a German hairdresser who had been a prisoner of war, Russians, Romanians and Polish Jews.

The chief listening set was at Sailly-Saillisel, east of Combles, installed in a cellar under the *château*, now a mound of earth and bricks. From there wires ran up to the front line and out into no man's land. There were wireless sets also at Lesboeufs, Morval and Combles.

I saw a lot of the old field company. They were still in the same camp in front of Trônes Wood. It was quite liveable now; the mud was no longer mud. There seemed to be very little for them to do either. Digging and earth work of any kind were now quite out of the question.

***

Every week the frost got heavier. Nothing like it had been known in the country before. By the beginning of February, the ground was frozen 3 feet down and any excavation had to be done with guncotton. The shell holes were filled with solid blocks of ice.

The troops and animals became grotesque objects. Breath froze on one's face in long icicles. Feet were encased in sandbags to prevent slipping on the icy trench-boards, for even now one had to keep to the tracks, as the deep snow hid crevasses and tangles of old barbed wire. Huge goat-skin jackets were issued to the troops so that they looked like Eskimos.

The caked mud on the horses and mules got frozen and stayed on them for months; one often saw a mule's tail with a ball of ice 5 or 6 inches in diameter, swinging on the end of it. Water carts froze solid and had to have fires lit under them whenever water was to be drawn.

At the water points, where water had to be kept running to prevent the main pipelines freezing, huge mounds of ice formed in strange shapes.

The effects of shelling also got much worse. Men were hit by flying splinters of ice and every shell burst on the surface, scattering the blast wider than normal.

***

15th February 1917

Suddenly the weather turned to warm wind and rain and in a few days, there was chaos. Hardly a road was fit for traffic. The surface broke up and left a spongy mass of thawing earth, into which lorries, caterpillars and wagons sank axle deep.

Up in the line the trenches were no longer recognisable, and the conditions of early December returned but far worse. After several days of warm rain, the weather improved and one looked for signs of spring. Over the whole hundred square miles of brown desert a pale green did appear, but it was a sort of false spring: a covering of filthy green slime that had hatched out in the first warm weather. In the pools of water in the shell holes, great masses of vivid coloured scum began to grow: some blood red, some purple, some yellow or green. The whole land seemed to have started rotting. The stink of bodies of men and horses – whose decomposition had been held up by the frost – filled the air.

***

About 20th February, we were awakened in the early morning by a curious noise like that of crackling holly magnified a thousand times. There was a red glare over in the direction of the Maricourt Dump about a quarter of a mile away. It was on fire. All the small stuff was going off merrily. Hundreds of tons of bombs, rifle ammunition and 18-pounder shells, burning and exploding furiously. No one could get near to it to do anything. Apparently, a Bosch plane had set it off with an incendiary bomb. There was nothing to do but wait for the inevitable. It was a very big dump containing all the reserve ammunition for the 14th and 15th Corps.

At last, at 10.00 am it happened. It was like a volcano erupting. There was an earthquake and an air blast that all but knocked one down as several thousand tons of big shells (up to 15 inches) all detonated together. A column of black and yellow smoke shot up 500 feet into the air and spread out like a mushroom, while lightning flashes played about in the ball of smoke at the top, lighting it up in vivid colours. For a mile around, the ground was covered with debris and the main road and the railway had to be closed for two days.

***

It was a few days after this that I went over to see Schon at 20th Division Headquarters near Trônes Wood. He was now Adjutant to Rolland, the CRE. The office staff were looking pale and scared and I was called aside and asked to try to persuade Schon to go to hospital. They said he was mad.

I got him to come for a long walk and finally convinced him that something was wrong and he then went away in an ambulance fairly happily [i.e. willingly]. Poor Schon. His old head wound received on the canal bank had produced some pressure on the brain. He was quite mad: he had a wonderful scheme for winning the war in a month and wanted to go straight to Cavan about it. His brain was working like an express train.

He lived in a padded cell for a year, but fortunately eventually recovered, although he never came out to the front again. He was the only officer in the old company whom I knew now; all the others had gone. After this I rather lost touch with them.

***

The first CW[90] wireless sets had just arrived and as the Bosch had started an almost continuous bombardment of Sailly-Saillisel, seriously interrupting communications with the forward battalions of the Guards Division who were holding the line there. We were told to install one in a dugout under Sailly church. This was to work back to [i.e. connect with] the other sets at the Brigade HQ behind Combles. The Bosch bombardment was kept up practically without stopping, day and night, and it was a difficult job carrying up batteries and stores for the forward set. Our listening station under the château further back was blown in and all the men there killed.

***

25th February 1917

Suddenly a report came in that the Bosch had begun to retire on the Ancre further north and three days later patrols reported the trenches opposite the 14th Corps front empty.

It was so unexpected. There was no longer any front line! People wearing cloth caps instead of the usual steel helmet wandered about over the German trenches, staring dazedly at the emptiness.

Very soon there were accidents. Booby traps had been left everywhere by the Bosch and these began to take effect. When trodden on, loose steps of dugouts released spring contacts that blew up the dugout; when pulled out in curiosity, an umbrella sticking up in a trench exploded a mine underneath. There were land mines under the roads and bombs in comfortable looking houses that attracted people to make billets of them; these had long time fuses so that they blew up weeks afterwards. At Étricourt, a masonry road bridge spanned the deep cutting of the Canal du Nord. It blew up in a few days and a temporary wooden bridge was put up on the old abutments. Three weeks afterwards the abutments themselves blew up!

The Bosch retired slowly and methodically for about a month, leaving behind a mere husk of the country, with every tree cut down and every house wrecked. A green wholesome country for all that with roads intact (except where the crossroads had been mined) and with all the signs of spring in the fields.

Towards the end of March, they were back in the Hindenburg Line and the retreat ceased. On the 8th March, I moved up to a dugout just behind Combles, with two of the cable section officers and on the 19th [March] to another dugout near Sailly.

About the 14th March, a curious thing happened. An old mine or store of explosives suddenly blew up under the camp where we had lived with the Guards Division field companies near Montauban in November; the very place we used to loose off cordite into the ground to smoke the rats out. Perhaps someone else had been doing the same thing. Anyhow there were dozens of men killed and a large mine-sized crater was left.

***

During April, the 14th Corps Headquarters handed over to another corps and withdrew to Méaulte. There was now very little to do. The Signal Company was employed chiefly in dismantling the maze of permanent line and cable that had been strewn over the old battlefield last year and was now left behind out of use.

The old battlefield was a weird place indeed. Even up to the middle of April, no blade of grass had appeared. Only the green and purple filth grew in the water in the shell holes, from which the rotting bodies of men and mules still protruded. Away from the roads, with a stream of traffic heading eastwards into the new country, it was absolutely deserted. There were a large areas, especially in and around the sites of former villages like Morval and Le Transloy, where no one had been since their capture months before. Half collapsed stairways led down to forgotten tunnels where the dead still rotted. Wreckage and broken vehicles lay about where they had been abandoned in the mud six months before.

At last the spring got the better of the poisoned ground. Cornflowers and poppies began to cover it, and a few weeks later an extraordinary weed sprang up everywhere over the whole country wherever the ground have been broken up by shells. How it got there nobody could explain. It grew furiously as in H.G. Wells' *Food of the Gods* and soon covered up everything.

On 6th April I went home on leave until the 16th [April].

***

April and May 1917

The campaign of 1917 had started on the 9th April with the Battle of Arras, which lasted until May, and the disastrous French attack on the Aisne on the 16th [April]. On the 5th April, too, the Americans came into the war.

Towards the end of May, the 14th Corps Headquarters left the Somme. We all went up north by lorry to Méteren, north-west of Armentières. On this front too there were great preparations for a big battle – an attack on the Messines Ridge – for which preparations had been made a year ago, in which the 20th Division might have taken part. There was still nothing for us to do. The 14th Corps were evidently not going to take any part in this show. The battle actually came off on 7th June, after a violent bombardment, and the springing of a series of huge mines, the shock of which could be felt in England.

***

15th June 1917

On the 15th June, I was posted away to the Cavalry Corps Signals, whose headquarters were at Catelet[91] a few miles south-east of Péronne, back in the Somme country again.

The Cavalry Corps of five divisions, two Indian and three British, were holding the line north of St Quentin as infantry. It was a very quiet sector and hardly a shell was fired. The Bosch were entrenched in the famous Hindenburg Line, behind wire hundreds of feet thick, so that both sides lay still and did nothing.

There was plenty of work for us to do, however. The Front was a wide one and there were lots of wireless sets, power buzzers and listening sets to be looked after.

The Cavalry Corps Signals were strange people. They had never taken any real part in the war. The cavalry had never been used as a corps by themselves until now, and even now it was the very quietest bit of the line they were holding. They were all regular officers and cavalrymen, except Trench the new AD Signals who had just taken the place of a strange man named Sadlier-Jackson.

My already low opinion of regular officers fell still more. They talked of nothing by going back to the Forest of Crécy for winter training. The sound of the guns came from very far away and they thanked God they were not as other men. Nothing mattered as long as their horses were fat and looked well and as long as their cars would keep going so that they could get away into Amiens or go round to yarn with their friends.

3rd July 1917

The Cavalry Corps were relieved by an infantry corps and went back again into the General Reserve for which they were heartily thankful.

During the next three weeks we tracked slowly north and finally fetched up at the village just south of Aire where we settled down for an apparently indefinite stay. There was nothing to do. Aire was a dirty town full of Portuguese troops.

The cavalry would never be used again. They were out of date and their minds were out of date. Meanwhile there were rumours of a great battle coming off to the north. I longed to be back near where things were happening. I regretted ever having left the old field company and joining the Signals. Finally, when the great bombardment started that made the whole country vibrate, and the cavalry started a compulsory pole parade for officers on Sunday mornings, I could stand it no longer.

On Sunday, 29th, I got on a motorbike and went to see Stratton, who used to be OC Signals in the 20th Division all the time I was in the 83rd Field Company. He was now a colonel and AD signals of the 19th Corps, which would be taking part in the battle. After a three-hour journey along the old road through Cassel and Poperinghe, I arrived at 19th Corps HQ at Nine Elms Camp, about a mile north of Poperinghe. Luckily, he was in and luckier still he was short of an officer. That afternoon he went off to the Fifth Army HQ at Lovie Château and fixed it all up.

31st July 1917

Two days later the 5th and 2nd Armies, with 500,000 troops, attacked in conjunction with the French on their left, from Boesinghe in the north to the Lys in the south. It was the opening of the great Battle of Passchendaele, and was preceded by five days and nights of the most intense bombardment of the war, by more than 6,000 guns from 18 pounder to 15 inch.

Even 25 miles back at Aire, all the ground and air were trembling and thumping, with that curious noise that can be felt and not quite heard. Day and night it went on, until it got into one's head like a fever.

Orders arrived for me on the 2nd August and next day I left and reported to Stratton at Ten Elms Camp just north of Poperinghe. For the third time I was back in the old area north of the Ypres Road. But now what a change. All the crops were trampled down, every field containing a camp or horse lines or a park of wagons.

Two great nations were deliberately pitting their whole concentrated national efforts against each other, all in a space a few miles wide. It was impossible to form much of an idea of what was going on as a whole. One had that overwhelming feeling of living in an enormous machine, working for one definite purpose.

In the drizzling mist the whistling of trains and the low hooting of light railways reminded one of the flat ground along the Thames near Woolwich. There was that curious noise of the traffic in London, that one hears on still, misty days. One couldn't go half a mile anywhere without coming upon one of the huge railway yards that were springing up, within a week, all over the place. They were the same old Southeastern engines and the same old English trucks; but they were all used now for one purpose. All the trucks were being unloaded of the same things: shells, road metal and timber.

Everything was changed in the Salient from what I had known before. The first ridge from Hooge to Pilckem had been captured, so that Ypres and the Country round the old Yser Canal was free from enemy observation. It seemed almost sacrilege to see lorries and locomotives right up near Bridge 6 on the canal bank. There were no machine guns to fire at you from the east bank. There were even lorries out on the Menin Road in broad daylight.

***

The 19th Corps Headquarters occupied a large camp of Nissen huts on one of the roads leading north from Poperinghe. Things had grown. The staff numbered 120 officers and Corps Signals had over twenty.

What a different atmosphere from the Cavalry Corps. Here everybody had a job and worked hard with one object in life: to get on with the war. There was a great battle going on and no time for any of the bickering and self-seeking that kept the cavalry people occupied.

Communications have never been so complex before or since. In the back areas up as far as Vlamertinghe, there was hardly a field without a great 40- or 100-line telephone route running through it. Hundreds of lines ran in a vast network between this centre and that. In each centre were little parties of 'line men', working in reliefs, day and night; sitting in huts and dugouts before great terminal boards, checking testing and changing over wires, as this main route and then that were cut by shell or aeroplane bomb.

Up in the forward area the complexity continued. Here the overhead routes [i.e. telephone wires] gave way to great bundles of multi-core cable, buried in the ground, and these ran between the signal dugouts. To each of these signal centres ran scores of communication lines: to batteries, infantry brigades, dressing, stations, ammunition, dumps, sound-ranging stations and what not. All of these ran their own telephone cables over the ground and were allotted lines on the main corps system.

Complicated and ever-changing records were kept at Corps Headquarters, but Stratton seemed to have the present allotment of every line in the whole vast system in his head. Every day some main arterial route would be cut down by shells or bombs, and always a little jet of soft, half inaudible orders from this amazing little Cambridge don who used to teach astronomy and mathematics would provide alternative communications for a whole group of Artillery, Brigades, Divisional Headquarters and a dozen other units and headquarters, so that the rush of thousands of messages and telephone conversations could carry on.

Even on the eve of the battle, when the most vital communications in the Corps completely broke down (owing to all the buried cables through the bottleneck of Ypres being blown up by big shells) and when almost at the same time, the officer on the spot and all his line men were killed by a mustard gas shell exploding in the dugout near the Dead End, there was no fuss. His plans for elaborate makeshift lines were all made up in a minute. Without looking at his records, he sat down to the telephone and detailed orders to various officers all over the corps area for an hour. This was after dinner one evening; by dawn, everything was normal again!

***

About the 10th August, I went over to the St Sixte Convent where the 14th Corps were living to see Colonel Mordaunt. Everyone one had ever known in the war who hadn't been knocked out seemed to be up in the little area of the Salient. The 20th Division were up north near Boesinghe. Mainsty was now staff officer to the chief engineer of the 19th Corps. Arundel Clay was in an engineers' company somewhere nearby.

I happened to return by Hamhoek Woods [to the north of Poperinghe], and there was the 10th Entrenching Battalion still in the same camp with the same funny old major commanding them.

On the 15th August, I went up to the big signal dugout at Potijze in readiness for a general attack by the whole 5th Army which took place on the morning of the 16th [August].

16th August 1917

Never have I heard or seen such a thing as that bombardment. The corps front only extended for a thousand yards on either side of the Potijze Road, and yet in that 2,000 yards there were more than 1,600 guns. They were nearly all behind us facing the mouth of our dugout and firing over our heads: 18 pounders within a few dozen yards of us, 6-inch howitzers, 60 pounders, 8-, 9.2-, 12- and 15-inch howitzers in row after row behind every broken hedge in endless array in the darkness right back to Vlamertinghe. Each gun firing out of the darkness every few seconds and all pointing towards us. It was like the end of the world. Dancing tongues of green and red fire spouting from the ground in every direction and a din that is beyond description.

There was a 60-pounder battery just behind that went off like pistol shots being fired into one's ear. If you tried to get away from it by getting into a deep dugout, it followed you with hammer blows like a punch following a nail into a hole.

In the odd pauses in the firing of the nearest batteries, one could hear the echoes of the last salvos in the ruined trees of Potijze Wood, and the overwhelming gurgling raw, like a great flood, of hundreds of huge howitzer shells passing high overhead.

Over there to the east on the Passchendaele Ridge, whole villages were being torn up by the roots and woods were disappearing. The courses of streams were being changed. Very soon the Bosch began to reply and added to the general pandemonium. The air heavy with burnt cordite now became loaded with the fumes of mustard gas.

Later on in the morning, the wounded began to stream down the Potijze Road to the dressing station next door to our dugout and soon the four doctors in shirtsleeves were covered in blood from head to foot like slaughtermen in a shambles.

***

26th August 1917

Shortly after this I took over the work on a new buried cable which was to be laid forward from the existing cable centre at St Jean, up over the first ridge past Wieltje and down into the valley of the Steenbeek.

It was really like the old days with the 83rd Field Company. I had a working party of two companies of a pioneer battalion, who were employed to dig the long 6-foot trench in which our own party of sappers lead the four 7-pair cables as carefully as darkness would allow.

It was nearly all night work. We used to leave by lorry an hour before dusk at about half past six, meet the working party at St Jean, collect the cable which had arrived during the evening in 1 cwt drums by light railway, and proceed up the road to where the end of the cable had got the previous night.

The front was now well to the east of the Steenbeek stream, whose course was almost blotted out by shell holes, leaving a vague swamp at the bottom of the valley the whole of which was in full view of the Bosch from the main Passchendaele Ridge.

We had a good many casualties and some nights it was impossible to work through the gas shelling. One of our officers, Miller I think his name was, a youngster just out from home, sat down in a shell hole for a minute and got so burnt with mustard gas which soaked into his clothes from the ground, that he eventually had to be sent home.

Sometimes in the early morning as the lorry took us back along the St Jean Road down the gentle hill past battery after battery of guns, one could see the gas in the dim dawn, hanging near the ground and slowly pouring like a grey oil down the hill from shell hole to shell hole, where the batteries had been shelled during the night.

NOTES

1 Ralph Alger Bagnold.
2 Sometimes abbreviated to RE.
3 Sometimes abbreviated to Coy.
4 Sometimes abbreviated to Div.
5 Ludendorff widely quoted e.g. by AJP Taylor *The First World War: An Illustrated History*, p.220
6 Kiggel widely quoted e.g. by AJP Taylor *The First World War: An Illustrated History*, p.148
7 The Shop, a euphemism for Royal Military Academy Woolwich.
8 A note on the varying use of capitalisations with the terms 'the front' and 'the line' in First World War literature. The Front as a shortened version of the Western Front is usually, though not always, capitalised. Informal descriptions of sections of the front line (e.g. the Laventie front) and the term 'the line' are more commonly written using lower case.
9 Railway Transport Officer.
10 Number.
11 Quartermaster's.
12 Making huts.
13 Sometimes abbreviated to EB.
14 Deputy Adjutant-General.
15 General Headquarters.
16 Entrenching Battalion.
17 i.e. Carrying much equipment, strapped to his upper body.
18 Today Flemish spellings of place names in northern Belgium have supplanted the French used during the First World War. Like everyone else R.A.B. used the terms and spellings in common use at the time and these have been preserved here e.g. Poperinghe (French) rather than Poperinge (Flemish) and Ypres (French) rather than Ieper (Flemish).
19 The term Bosch predates the First World War. Derived from the Turkish *boş*, meaning 'empty', it was used in British English from the 1830s to mean 'absurd or foolish talk, nonsense or rubbish': an apt term reused to describe an enemy viewed with contempt. Curiously the French also used the term *Boche* to describe the Germans in the First World War, the French slang being a shortened form of *portmanteau alboche*, itself derived from a hybrid of *Allemand* ('German') and *caboche* ('head' or 'cabbage'). While its use may seem bigoted to us today, it should simply be taken as a substitute for 'German' or 'enemy'.
20 Small cafés.
21 Fortified positions.
22 Royal Military College, Kingston, Ontario.
23 Binoculars.

24 Thin yet tough and flexible willow branches used for wattle constructions.
25 i.e. Closer to the front line.
26 Reinforce.
27 '...with binding wire to pickets' is an odd phrase to modern ears. R.A.B. is describing a sort of picket fence construction used to strengthen trench walls.
28 Sometimes abbreviated to Bde.
29 An example of the men setting themselves up as impromptu groups of field entertainers.
30 Commanding Royal Engineers i.e. the commanding engineer officer in a given locality.
31 Headquarters.
32 Officer Commanding.
33 Sometimes abbreviated to Lieut.
34 Refuse heap.
35 Presumably a store near the front line.
36 Canadian Pacific Railway.
37 Revetting: latticed framework, made from interwoven wood, meant to shore up trench walls.
38 So called because of their inadequacy.
39 General Officer Commanding.
40 Deride.
41 Quartermaster Sergeant.
42 Mills bomb or hand grenade.
43 Sometimes abbreviated to Sgt.
44 King's Royal Rifles (complete regimental name: The King's Royal Rifle Corps)
45 An excruciating and racist phrase by modern standards. In the language of the time, it was a common euphemism for 'worked extremely hard' and is, of course, linked to the harshness of slave labour.
46 A device to determine the level/flatness of land.
47 i.e. Strengthened against a bursting shell.
48 Non-commissioned officers.
49 i.e. Ticking-off.
50 General Service.
51 A break – literally a pause to catch one's breath.
52 Assistant Provost Marshal.
53 A detached house or villa rather than a gambling house.
54 *Pavé* is a type of cobbled road particular to the Low Countries.
55 A Dutch/Flemish word, translating to 'inn' or 'hostel' in English.
56 R.A.B. habitually uses a capital C for the 'Canal' as it is the shortened form of Yser Canal. However, this starts to look rather overdone on the page, so this transcription uses the lower case 'canal' throughout.
57 Almost exactly ten months before.
58 21st–23rd February 1916.
59 Renewed anxiety.
60 Durham Light Infantry.
61 Whiz-bang (or whizz-bang): a small-calibre, high-velocity shell.
62 A low, temporary defence or parapet.
63 Second Lieutenant Dalgas was in fact Danish.
64 R.A.B. switches between Brigadier Butler and General Butler, reflecting the classification of brigadiers at the time in the British Army as the lowest of the general officer rank. Brigadiers, sometimes referred to by the full title brigadier general, were one below major general. After the First World War, brigadier was reclassified as a field officer rank.

65 Blastine: a high-explosive compound.
66 Lieutenant.
67 Division.
68 The double exclamation marks, almost certainly inserted by R.A.B., implicitly mark *his* incredulity.
69 Sir William Beach Thomas, British journalist and war correspondent working for the *Daily Mail* during the First World War.
70 The 38th Welsh Division began its assault on Mametz Wood on 7th July, taking it after grievous losses on the 12th. On 20th/21st (?) July the poet Robert Graves, serving with the Royal Welch Fusiliers, was badly wounded nearby at Bazentin churchyard. As Graves recounts in *Goodbye to All That* he was mistakenly recorded as having 'died of wounds', the erroneous message reaching his parents in a letter from his CO dated 22nd July and additionally reported in *The Times*. However, he survived and lived to be ninety. Approximately a mile to the west of Mametz Wood is Contalmaison, which at the start of the Somme offensive lay behind the German lines. By early August the remains of this village had been taken in the British advance. Today Contalmaison Château Cemetery is the final resting place of Private William Henry Short VC, my wife Karen's great uncle, who – after conspicuous courageous action – died of wounds at Contalmaison dressing station on the night of 6th/7th August 1916.
71 Distinguished Service Order
72 R.A.B.'s expression 'gas helmet' puts the modern reader in mind of a metal helmet, which was not the case. However, the term was widely used by British troops in the First World War to describe the 'PH Helmet', which consisted of a soft material, gas-permeable hood, the flannel lining of which was treated with Phenate Hexamine, counteracting the effects of chlorine, phosgene and tear gases.
73 Rifle Brigade.
74 Who became Edward VIII in 1936 and abdicated the same year.
75 6eme Armée.
76 While such comments mark R.A.B. as dismissive, even contemptuous of the Irish, he harboured no notable animosity for them, and it should be remembered that he remarks much earlier in the memoir: 'They were an awfully nice lot of fellows. All Irishmen.' We should recognise, however, that it was probably not uncommon at the time for English people to regard the Irish as somewhat 'wild', certainly different in temperament to themselves. It is also significant that the Easter Uprising in Ireland had occurred less than five months previously. R.A.B. served in Ireland with the British Army during the early 1920s during the Civil War yet chose to honeymoon there after the Second World War.
77 Maconochie: a canned British stew of sliced turnips, carrots, potatoes, onions, haricot beans, and beef in a thin broth, named after the Aberdeen-based Maconochie Company that produced it.
78 The *Briqueterie* (French for brickworks) was a German defensive strongpoint located approximately 100 yards south of the crossroads near Bernafay Wood and just south-east of the village of Montauban. It was a key objective for the first day of the Battle of the Somme (1st July 1916) and one of the very few objectives taken on that day.
79 Raymond Herbert Asquith, Grenadier Guards, son of the then prime minister Herbert Henry Asquith. Raymond Asquith was killed in action near Ginchy on the 15th September 1916 and is buried at Guillemont Road Cemetery.
80 i.e. Fairer.
81 Distress signal.

82 Different in some way, one presumes, from the 29th Division's red triangle.
83 Marked as a hamlet about a mile east of Combles on R.A.B.'s map. No such place exists today – one can only assume it was never rebuilt.
84 Expeditionary Force Canteen.
85 One shirking military service.
86 Sir Eric Campbell Geddes, politician who served as head of Military Transportation on the Western Front, with the rank of major-general.
87 The Royal Engineers Signals Service was formed in 1908. The Royal Corps of Signals came into being in 1920.
88 R.A.B. is likely referring to a 'forty-and-eight boxcar', a railway carriage which transported either forty men or eight horses.
89 Assistant Director.
90 Continuous Wave.
91 This is R.A.B.'s spelling. Looking at a map of the area today, there is no Catelet in this position, although there is a Le Catelet some 18 miles east-north-east of Péronne. Would this not have been behind the German lines in June 1917? Perhaps the Catelet of which R.A.B. spoke was obliterated.

BIBLIOGRAPHY

Books

Bagnold, Ralph A., (1990), *Sand, Wind and War*, University of Arizona Press, Tuscon

Faulks, Sebastian, (1993), *Birdsong*, Hutchinson, London

Graves, Robert, (1929), *Goodbye to All That*, Jonathan Cape, London

Keegan, John, (1998) The First World War, Hutchinson, London

Remarque, Erich, (1929) *All Quiet on the Western Front*, originally published as *Im Westen nichts Neues*, Ullstein Verlag, Berlin

Taylor, A. J. P., (1963), *The First World War: An Illustrated History*, Hamish Hamilton, London

Interviews

R.A.B.'s interview with the Imperial War Museum (1990)

Poems

Sassoon, Siegfried, 'The General'

Illustrative Material

All photographs and maps are credited to the individual copyright holder.

INDEX

Named Personnel

Place name, Belgium

Place name, Belgium-France

Place name, France

Place name, France (Somme)